YOU DON'T HAVE TO BELIEVE THAT

DISEMPOWER YOUR NEGATIVE THOUGHTS AND LIVE WITH FREEDOM

MANISH PABARI

macpabari@gmail.com

First Edition August 2022

ISBN: 978-1-7396063-0-5

To my parents, my partner and my daughter
for your unconditional love and support.

(Personal) reality is merely an illusion, albeit a very persistent one.

Albert Einstein

CONTENTS

PART FOUR - THE EXTRAS
Putting It Into Practice

INTRODUCTION

My name is Manish Pabari. I am a professional coach, 50 years old, a single child of loving parents, with a beautiful teenage daughter of my own and a wonderfully supportive life partner. I am grateful to be living an emotionally peaceful life, filled with rewarding work and thriving relationships.

But life hasn't always been this good...

Seven years ago (in 2015), my marriage of fifteen years was breaking down. Prior to our separating, I wanted to spend as much time as possible with my daughter. So I decided to quit my corporate job to become a full-time dad. Whilst my daughter was at school, I devoted my time to training to become a coach. It took me some time to build up the courage to make these reasonably dramatic life changes. I recall experiencing daunting thoughts about the possible impact on my daughter, the financial uncertainty that a career change and divorce would bring, and of how my wife might react. Amidst these unsettling thoughts, I remember having moments of clarity, when making these changes seemed like the obvious thing to do and it was in one of these moments that I decided to take a step into the unknown.

At first, it didn't quite work out the way I had hoped. After officially separating from my wife in 2016, I found myself alone in Sydney, Australia, with my daughter having moved to another state (Melbourne) with her mother. I had no other family in the continent and had to reinvent my friendship circle. This lasted for two years and, at times, I was very lonely. It was, however, also a period when I began reading books in search of answers about the nature of our human experience. I wanted to understand *why we feel the way we do*.

I adopted an approach of *learning* through reading, *applying* what I learnt to my own life and then *sharing* with clients, family and friends. I found this approach invaluable and continue to do so today. It helped me to drive transformation in my professional and personal life that I could not have imagined possible.

I spent the first twenty-one years of my working life as an investment manager working at some of the world's largest insurance companies. I now work as a coach supporting people to achieve peak performance in their working lives, improving their relationships with others and themselves, and enhancing their enjoyment of life in general.

When I'm not working as a coach you will find me volunteering for multiple organisations including Childline (taking calls from young people struggling with some aspect of their lives), running well-being workshops for school children and staff, and teaching financial literacy.

In this book, I would like to share some insights on how

we experience life, that have helped me so much; in particular, to provide a deeper understanding of the following statements:

- *All (yes, all) the negative emotions in our lives come from made-up thoughts, that do not have to be believed.*

- *Our happiness is built-in, and is not linked to what we achieve, do, are or think.*

The aim of this book is to help you make your life more enjoyable, with less time spent in negative emotions and more time in peace and a sense of freedom. Success is a by-product of being in this state. You will find practical suggestions to help guide you. This book contains many concepts, so you may want to read it in stages and digest the ideas before you move on. If you, like me, cannot relate to some of the concepts at first, that's okay. Don't be surprised if your intellect tries to dismiss some of the ideas, as they may challenge some strongly held beliefs. All I ask is that you keep an open mind to trying these approaches to see how they work for you. What I am about to share has transformed my life in a magical way. I hope that it will do the same for you.

With all my love, Manish

OUR PATH TOGETHER

For a large part of my life, I believed that my external circumstances had a significant influence on my happiness and how I felt at any given moment. I thought that studying hard, securing a good job, getting married, buying a nice house, having kids, were the key to a happy life. Yet, having achieved all of this, happiness seemed to come and go from one moment to the next without any direct link to my circumstances.

But as I will explain, I now realise that our emotions (feelings) are directly linked to our thinking in that moment and not our external circumstances. In essence, we are experiencing our lives from the inside-out (via thought), instead of from the outside-in (via circumstance).

Furthermore, I have also come to understand that we cannot control our thoughts all of the time and, importantly, our thoughts are not the truth; they are made-up. The only truth is whatever is happening in that moment, without the filter of personal interpretation. Once we appreciate that our thoughts are made-up and cannot be controlled, we can choose not to believe our thinking, especially when our thoughts are creating negative feelings.

In the first part of this book, 'The Story Of How We Experience Life', we will explore all of this in more detail to provide you with a deeper understanding of how the mind creates our experience of life. But this understanding is only the beginning of our journey. Next, we will delve into the link between thinking, happiness and performance.

Contrary to what many believe, happiness is built-in to all of us. It is intrinsic to the kindness of the design of being human. The only thing that takes us away from being happy, is believing our judgemental thinking. As you learn to trust this beautiful gift of your body and mind, to do exactly what it needs, when it needs, peak performance becomes more effortless and life becomes more enjoyable regardless of your starting point. You also start taking your thinking less seriously.

By accepting whatever is happening right now, we show unconditional love for ourselves as well as for others, and we see that our happiness is not linked to what we achieve, do, are or think; happiness is always at hand. Even lousy feelings are part of the kindness of the design, as they are telling us not to trust our thinking in that moment and let those thoughts pass. As these lousy thoughts pass, our mind tends to quieten. And in this quiet, space is made for more inspiring, creative and enjoyable thoughts to enter.

In part two, 'The Beauty, The Kindness of the Design', we will look at why we can trust ourselves, how our default is to be happy, and finding our way back to happiness when we get lost, including ways to quiet the mind.

Everyone feels lousy sometimes. This is just a part of how we experience life. What so many of us don't realise is that these negative feelings usually stem from believing some form of judgemental thinking. We all have a judge in our head. In part three of this book, 'The Drama, Instruments of the Judge', we will look at some of the instruments often used by our inner judge to create negative feelings. I will highlight ways to catch the judge in action and thereby avoid staying in that state of negative feeling for as long.

In the final part of this book, 'The Extras, Putting It Into Practice', we will look at how this understanding—that we are *feeling our thinking* at all times; that *thoughts are made-up*, so they *do not have to be believed*—can be applied to enhance everyday situations in our lives, whether that relates to personal performance or love and relationships.

I have deliberately tried to keep the language in this book as simple as possible. This is so that the book can be read by someone of any age, young or old.

As I developed my understanding of how we experience life, I had many questions. No doubt you will also have the same. So I have written this book in a questions and answers format with the hope to provide many answers.

PART ONE

THE STORY

Of How We Experience Life

All you have to know is everything is created from thought, you don't have to know anything else.

Sydney Banks

CHAPTER 1

WE ARE CONSTANTLY FEELING OUR THINKING

Imagine you are at home on your own on a Sunday afternoon. You have spent most of the day cleaning the house. You have just made a cup of tea, sat down on the sofa and put your feet up, ready to catch up on your favourite television show. You are feeling relaxed, as your work is done for the day. A few minutes into watching your show, you remember that next week, work is going to be really busy with a number of deadlines approaching. The relaxed feeling soon disappears. Now you feel quite anxious and stressed about the week ahead. Your attention is suddenly caught by a touching moment on the television, which brings a smile to your face. In that moment, you have forgotten about the work deadlines and are feeling relaxed again. It occurs to you that in the space of a few minutes, whilst sitting on the sofa, you have gone from feeling relaxed to anxious, and then back to relaxed. You then begin to wonder...

Where do our feelings come from?

Our whole experience of life, moment to moment, comes from our thinking, not our circumstances!

For all of us, our experience of life is shaped by our emotions in that moment. Our emotions (also called feelings) are very real and are experienced internally and sometimes through our bodies as physical sensations. And at all times, the source of our feelings is our thinking, rather than our circumstances.

Take a moment to digest this, because, like me, you may not believe this at first. Pause and observe what you are thinking and feeling right now. Then wait for a new thought to appear and see how that changes the way you feel. You are *feeling your thinking* from moment to moment.

Put another way, there is a direct link between feeling and thought. There is no direct link between feeling and circumstance.

Thought ⇨ Feeling

How can you prove that you are feeling your thinking in that moment?

In the example above, the feelings changed with no significant change in circumstance. The feelings changed as the thoughts went from a sense of accomplishment having completed the housework (feeling relaxed), to work deadlines (feeling stressed) and then to the touching moment on the television (feeling relaxed).

I'm sure there have been times in your life when people appear to have different feelings even though their circumstances are exactly the same. I've seen it on many occasions on the London Underground, for example. When a train is delayed, some people get visibly annoyed, yet others accept that the delays are out of their control and don't seem bothered. This reinforces the idea that we are feeling our own thoughts, as opposed to the circumstances.

Have you ever been in the same situation more than once, but felt completely different each time? The situation hasn't changed, but you feel different, because your thinking has changed. It happens to me whilst playing tennis. Usually, I am pretty relaxed as I think of it as just a game and know that I am playing for fun. But on occasion, I take it more seriously and false shots feel more frustrating.

Sometimes our circumstances seem to have no bearing on our thoughts and the corresponding feelings they create, like when we are daydreaming. I often observe my daughter munching on her breakfast, lost in her own thoughts and smiling. She may be thinking about her day ahead and spending time with her friends at school. The point is that the circumstance (having breakfast in this case) has no impact on how she is feeling in that moment. In fact, when she is daydreaming, anything I say to her would simply fall on deaf ears.

All of these examples point to how our feelings are driven by our thinking in that moment, not our circumstances.

But surely, my external circumstances can affect how I am feeling, right?

I understand how our circumstances may look like they affect how we are feeling, but there is no direct link between feelings and circumstances.

Our thoughts can be (and often are) influenced by our circumstances. For example, you may be unwell physically and this could lead to worries about your health. It is understandable that being ill could get you down, but there are many people who have long-term illnesses and yet they do not let it get to them.

How you are feeling always depends on how you are thinking about the situation. In other words, we do not experience our circumstance, we experience our thinking of the circumstance.

Circumstance ⇨ Thought ⇨ Feeling

But when I am faced with a difficult circumstance, I get anxious and I feel this anxiety in my body. This anxious feeling seems very real. Doesn't this mean that I am feeling my circumstance?

Yes, our feelings are very real and we often experience them through our body. Imagine you are about to go into the examination room for your final mathematics exam at high school. You find mathematics really difficult.

You don't think that you are well prepared and you are worried that you might mess up the exam. The palms of your hands are sweaty and your legs are trembling. In fact, you feel a general sense of nervousness throughout your body. These physical sensations are certainly real and you believe that these sensations are because of your exam.

However, would you feel the same way if you did not think that maths was 'difficult' and you were not having the worrying thoughts about messing up the exam? Chances are, you would feel very differently if you thought that maths was 'easy' and, instead of worrying, you were focused on doing the best you can with the knowledge and understanding of maths that you have. With these more empowering thoughts, you are likely to feel calmer and more relaxed about the exam.

In this situation, the thought (maths is difficult) created the feeling (worry) which also manifested as physical sensations (sweaty hands, legs trembling, general nervousness throughout the body).

Thought ⇨ Feeling ⇨ Physical sensations

So, no, you are never feeling your circumstance, you are feeling your thinking of the circumstance. The fact that you experience your feelings as physical sensations through your body does not change this.

Sometimes I feel physical sensations of stress and I am not thinking about anything in particular. How can I be feeling my thinking if I don't know what I am thinking?

We all have so many thoughts passing through us that, sometimes, we do not recognise which thoughts are creating our feelings in that moment. For instance, you may feel a general sense of anxiety throughout your body and do not know why you are feeling this way. These feelings may be uncomfortable and you may be thinking 'I don't like this feeling' and asking 'why am I feeling this way?'. The discomfort of *not knowing why* and *not being able to accept this uncertainty*, both of which are thought created, may be causing the stressful feelings to continue.

In this case, the physical sensations (anxiety throughout body) created thoughts ('I don't like this' and 'why am I feeling this way?') which led to further feelings of anxiety.

If we were able to accept that sometimes we will feel physical sensations in our body and not know why, then we would, most likely, cease to feel anxious.

Here the order of events was:

Physical sensations ⇨ Thought ⇨ Feeling

Notice that thoughts always precede feelings, even when physical sensations are involved.

You are always feeling your thinking in that moment, but sometimes you may not recognise or notice which thoughts are creating your feelings.

Surely, my five senses create feelings and these are not thought created?

You may think that our five senses—sight, hearing, smell, taste and touch—generate feelings. However, our senses do not have a direct link to our feelings.

The senses pass through our thoughts to create feelings.

Senses ⇨ Thought ⇨ Feeling

You may see a bunch of red roses at a flower stall on Valentine's Day. You stop and smell them and think 'what beautiful flowers'. This thought will most likely create pleasant feelings, but notice here that the *thought* about the flowers being beautiful, preceded the feelings. Alternatively, you may have a completely different thought like 'I hope my wife doesn't expect flowers today, they are overpriced and a waste of money'. This will create completely different (less pleasant) feelings. In this example, two of your senses (sight and smell) created very different feelings depending on your thinking in that moment.

For clarity, when I say that you are feeling your thinking, I am not referring to our sense of feel (or touch). Touch is one of our five senses and is different to the feelings (emotions) that we experience. In the roses example above, we may feel (touch) the soft red flowers and this is different to the feelings that we experience through our thinking (about the flowers) in that moment.

How is it useful to me to know that I am feeling my thinking?

Understanding that we are constantly feeling our thinking can be liberating, as we are then no longer a victim of our circumstances. We begin to see that any drama (negative emotions) in our lives comes from our thinking, not from our circumstances. We also start to see that any lousy (negative) feelings are a direct result of lousy thinking (more on this later).

Our mind creates thoughts which are brought to life by our feelings

This is the essence of how we experience life. As our thoughts change, our feelings change. This happens constantly. As you begin to see the truth of this statement, you start to see that you are experiencing life from the inside-out (via thought), as opposed to the outside-in (via circumstance).

KEY INSIGHTS

Our whole experience of life is shaped by our feelings (emotions) from moment to moment.

Feelings are very real and are felt internally and sometimes through our bodies as physical sensations.

At all times, we are 'feeling our thinking' in that moment, not our circumstances.

There is a direct link between feeling and thought.

There is no direct link between feeling and circumstance, nor feeling and physical sensations, nor feeling and our senses.

We are experiencing life from the inside-out (via thought), as opposed to the outside-in (via circumstance).

EXERCISE

As you go through the next seven days, say, observe what thoughts pop up in your head and how you then feel. Write down your thoughts and corresponding feelings. This will build up your awareness of how you are *feeling your thinking*, not your circumstances.

CHAPTER 2

YOU DON'T HAVE TO BELIEVE THAT THOUGHT, IT'S MADE-UP!

Why do we have lots of different types of thoughts?

As humans we have a heart that pumps blood around our body, a stomach that digests food, kidneys that remove waste and extra fluid from our body and so on. It's part of being human and alive. Most of us never question why our organs perform these functions, we simply accept that they do.

In much the same way, we have an organ called the mind (or the brain) that creates thoughts. This is just how the mind works. We hear our thoughts through an 'inner voice' and we hear them almost all the time. You will hear this inner voice for your entire life.

This inner voice appears to give a running commentary on your life. Sometimes, it is very encouraging and compliments what you are doing. At other times, this voice is downright negative and is criticising you, telling you that what you did is not good enough. Sometimes, you are fully focused on a task and the inner voice is quiet.

Research from Queen's University in Canada and the Cleveland Clinic in America suggest that our minds actually create between 6,000 to 60,000 thoughts every day. This can equate to almost one thought every second! Some of these will be new thoughts, but many will be old, repeated thoughts. You will not even notice many of these thoughts as they pass through your mind, as you will be in 'automatic' mode. When we wake up in the morning how many of us notice the thought that says 'brush your teeth'? And yet we do it anyway.

If I am feeling my thinking at all times, should I try to change to think positively at all times?

Our lives would most likely be wonderful if we could change our thinking to only create positive thoughts. But this implies that we can control and direct our thinking all of the time. Let's consider if this is possible.

Do you think that you can control your thoughts all of the time? Try a little thought experiment. Put this book down for sixty seconds and observe what thoughts pop into your head during this time.

Could you control and direct all your thoughts? My guess is that you did not choose all the thoughts that came up in the sixty seconds. Some may have been influenced by your environment (what is around you). Some you may have chosen based on what you were focused on. However, some thoughts will have just appeared involuntarily.

The truth is that *we cannot control our thoughts all of the time.*

I mean, if you were unable to control your thoughts for just sixty seconds, imagine trying to control your thoughts all of the time. And if you can't control your thoughts all of the time, then it is impossible to always think positively. So trying to change to become a permanently, or even mostly, 'positive thinker' would be a waste of energy.

What can I do about my negative thoughts?

We all have negative (let's call them 'lousy') thoughts from time to time. This is just how the mind works. And it's okay to have lousy thoughts. It doesn't mean that there is anything wrong with you. You cannot stop them from coming.

However, I've never met anyone who actually wants to have lousy thoughts that make them feel lousy. No-one would reasonably choose to feel this way.

The good news is that we all have a powerful gift. This is the gift of *choice*. You may not be able to control all of your thoughts, but you can choose not to believe them, especially when they are lousy. Take a moment to reflect on this.

Your thoughts ⇨ cannot control ⇨ don't have to believe

Understanding this one thing, that *you don't have to believe that thought*, can transform your experience of life.

You do not have to change or stop your negative thoughts. In fact, you can't in any sustainable way. But you do not have to believe them. And choosing not to believe something might be easier when you know that it is out of your control.

Consider this: You have a friend whom you see frequently. You get on with them mostly, but sometimes, this friend says negative things to you. You may get upset when they do this, but you know that you don't have to believe everything that they say. After all, you cannot control what they say. Now imagine that this friend is your 'inner voice'. Does it make sense to believe everything that your inner voice says when you cannot control it?

What if my thoughts are true?

I was once coaching a teenage boy who was struggling to deal with his negative thoughts. I talked to him about how the mind creates thoughts, lots of them. I took him through the exercise of observing his thoughts for sixty seconds to help him see that he cannot control all of his thoughts. We then discussed how, if you cannot control your thoughts, then you don't have to believe them. All of this made sense to him, but then he asked 'but what if my thoughts are true?'. I paused to reflect on this seemingly simple, yet powerful question. After a few moments, I responded:

The *truth* can be defined as an accurate, objective reflection of events, which cannot be disputed. The truth does not change.

Now, it seems to me that our thoughts about an event can change over time. In other words, they are a subjective, personal interpretation of events. The truth cannot change. So, our thoughts cannot be the truth. They are made-up.

Take, for example, a couple who married on 1st March 2016. The couple greatly enjoyed their wedding day and, at the time, had wonderful thoughts about the day. But, unfortunately, a few years later, the relationship went sour and the couple decided to separate. Their thoughts of their wedding day became very different and not so wonderful. Their thoughts about the same event (their wedding day) have changed, so their thoughts cannot be the truth.

There are a number of factors pointing to thoughts being made up and not being true:

- Thoughts are not controllable by you at all times.
- No-one would reasonably choose to have lousy thoughts.
- Thoughts change constantly, at a speed of up to one new thought every second, which cannot all be true.
- Having different thoughts about the same

event. The truth about an event does not change, yet your thoughts about that same event can change.

- Thoughts are mostly a subjective interpretation of events, the truth is objective.

This helped the teenage boy see that what he thinks is made-up (a subjective, personal interpretation of events). Thoughts are not the truth (something that is objective, unchanging and indisputable).

The *truth* is simply whatever is happening in that moment, without any personal interpretation. For example, if it is raining then 'it is raining right now' is the truth. 'I hate it when it rains' is made-up. Or a friend did not turn up at your party then 'she did not come to my party' is the truth. 'She did not come to my party, because she is mad at me' is made-up. The only time our thinking is not made-up is when it is giving an accurate, objective account of whatever is happening right now, without any additional personal interpretation.

Once you understand that what you think is made-up, then not believing what you think, especially when it makes you feel lousy, seems a reasonable choice to make.

If this is the first time that someone has suggested that your thoughts are made-up, then you may well reject this idea initially. I have seen this many times when coaching clients. Some clients feel that it is an attack on their intellect, saying that their thoughts are made-up. To be clear, I am not saying that thoughts are useless. Thoughts are where wonderful ideas, creativity, wisdom and kindness all come from. But even these inspirational thoughts are made-up. The value in seeing the made-up nature of thought is that you can then pick and choose which thoughts to believe. You can then enjoy, and possibly act on, the inspiring thoughts and not believe the lousy ones.

If you are still not convinced that thoughts are made-up, all I ask is that you keep an open mind to the possibility, and see what happens to your experience of life as a result.

But it's hard not to believe my thinking, even if I understand that it is made-up. Why is this?

I get that it can be hard not to believe your thinking (your inner voice), it can be very persistent. I also understand that your thoughts can seem very real, because when you believe them, they turn into feelings, and feelings are very real. We can all get caught up in a whirlwind of negative thoughts from time to time, which create unwanted feelings of stress and distress.

But as your understanding deepens, that you are feeling your thinking and that your thoughts are made-up, it becomes easier not to believe your lousy thoughts. The purpose of this book is to help you strengthen this understanding and spend less time in unwanted negative feelings. Throughout this book we will look at various ways to increase your level of awareness so that you can recognise the made-up nature of thought quickly and more easily.

KEY INSIGHTS

The mind creates lots of different types of thoughts (positive and negative), at a speed of up to one new thought every second. You will not even notice many of these thoughts as you will be in automatic mode.

You cannot control your thoughts all of the time, so trying to become a permanently, or even mostly, positive thinker would be a waste of energy.

We all have negative thoughts from time to time. This is okay and does not mean that there is anything wrong with you.

You cannot change or stop your negative thoughts, but you can choose not to believe them.

The truth is an accurate, objective reflection of events, which cannot be disputed. The truth does not change.

The truth is whatever is happening in that moment, without any personal interpretation.

Your thoughts are a subjective, personal interpretation of events, which can change.

Your thoughts are made-up.

It can be hard not to believe your thoughts, because when you believe them, they turn into feelings, and feelings are real.

As your understanding deepens, that you are feeling your thinking and that your thoughts are made-up, it becomes easier not to believe your lousy thoughts and you spend less time in unwanted negative feelings.

EXERCISE

To help recognise the made-up nature of thought, here's an exercise for you to try as often as you like. When you are about to watch some television, hold off from turning on the television for ten minutes. During this time, sit back, relax and observe what thoughts pop into your head. Notice how many different thoughts come up. Notice how you cannot control all of them. Observe how your thoughts are like a storytelling machine full of subjective interpretations, almost as if you are watching a television show (without the television turned on). Notice how some thoughts feel very real (when you believe them), whereas you are able to dismiss other thoughts easily.

The more you do this exercise of observing your thoughts, the more you will notice how your thinking is made-up.

CHAPTER 3

NO THOUGHT IS HARMFUL BY ITSELF

Does every thought I have turn into a feeling?

We have already discussed how our thoughts are brought to life by our feelings. But not all thoughts create feelings. Remember, our thoughts can change from one second to the next. If every thought created a feeling, that would be a lot of changing feelings!

From what I've learnt, our thoughts are actually harmless and are only brought to life, through feelings, when:

1. We believe them, or
2. They grab our attention

But when our level of awareness is high and we understand that we are feeling our thinking in that moment, we can choose which thoughts to believe. If we don't enjoy the thoughts, then we don't have to believe them.

I don't understand. What do you mean 'when our level of awareness is high, we can choose which thoughts to believe'?

Imagine a constant stream of trains passing through a station. We're waiting at the station platform. When a train arrives, we either board it, or let it pass through. If we board the train, then we will go on a journey and experience varied scenery depending on the train's route. If we choose not to board, then that train will pass and we experience nothing from it.

Now, as the illustration below shows, imagine that your mind is the train station and your thoughts are trains passing through. If you board a train (believe a thought) that arrives at the station (your mind), then you will go on a journey (experience feelings) based on where the train (thought) takes you. If you do not board the train (do not believe a thought), then you will experience nothing from that train (thought) and it will just pass through.

Sometimes our level of awareness is low (we forget that we are feeling our thinking), and we may believe a thought that makes us feel lousy. But as our level of awareness rises and we understand that the lousy feeling has come from believing a lousy thought, we can choose not to believe that thought, let it pass and wait for a new thought to appear.

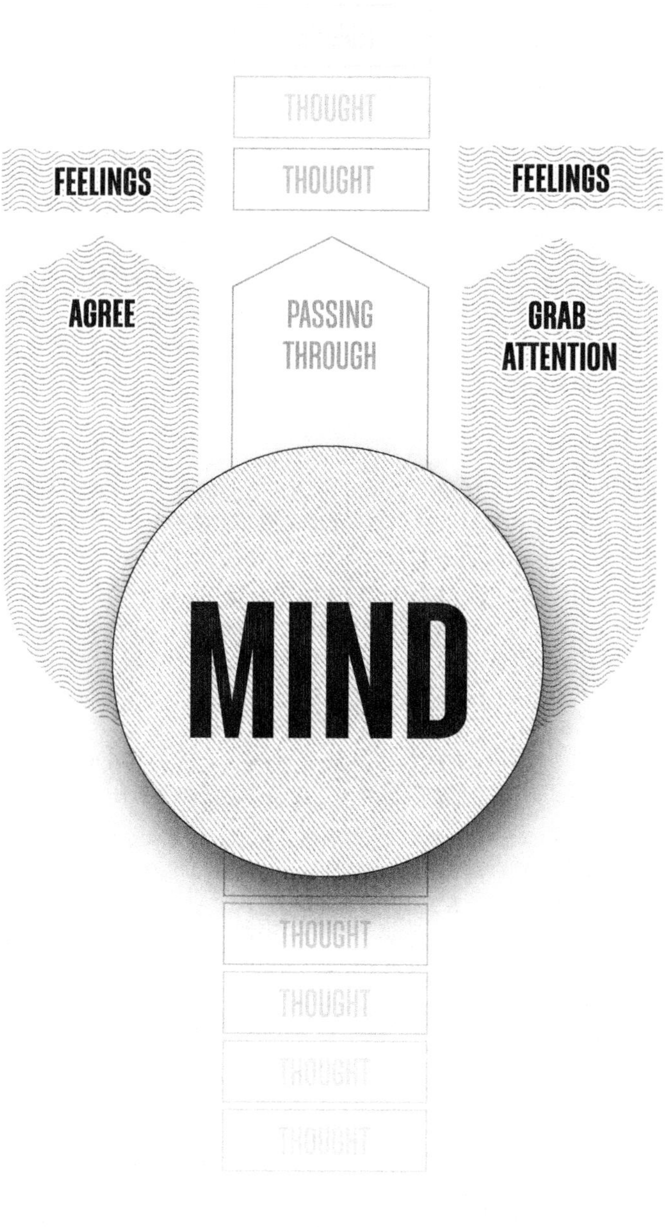
THOUGHT
THOUGHT
FEELINGS
FEELINGS
AGREE
PASSING THROUGH
GRAB ATTENTION
MIND
THOUGHT
THOUGHT

Sometimes, thoughts grab our attention and create negative feelings. We cannot always control which thoughts grab our attention, but when our awareness is working well we are able to recognise that it is the lousy thought that has created the negative feeling. This helps to let the thought pass. We may unintentionally board that lousy train (thought) but with our awareness high, we can choose to get off that train and let it pass. Our awareness (understanding that we are feeling our thinking) can act as a filter to let thoughts pass through our mind.

For example, I could have the thought that 'I'm not a good father'. This thought by itself is harmless and has no impact on my feelings unless I believe it. I happen to believe that I'm a pretty cool father, although you'd be better off asking my daughter if she agrees! Even if I don't believe this thought, if I start giving it attention by disagreeing with it, trying to dismiss it, or trying to stop it from appearing, then it is likely to keep coming back.

Should I try to make my negative thoughts go away?

As we have already explored, we cannot control all of our thinking, so there's not much point in trying to make a thought go away. But what I have experienced is that if we don't believe a thought, then it seems to disappear more easily making space for a new thought to pop up. When a thought appears that you're not enjoying, try not to put effort into making it go away, as this is giving the thought attention. The same thought may return, but the less attention you give it (by not believing it), the less often it is likely to return.

But I am really not enjoying my negative thoughts. What can I do when I am not enjoying my thoughts?

Here's the thing about thoughts. They are constantly changing. Therefore, *we are only one new thought away from a new experience (a new feeling)*. We do not need to do anything to change our thinking. Our thoughts and therefore, our feelings, will change naturally.

If you are troubled by negative thoughts, you may find it useful to treat your thoughts like a movie. A movie can appear very real when you are watching it, but once it is over, you know that it was just a movie. Imagine how you would feel if you knew that all your emotions were sourced from a movie (of made-up thoughts). Then you could let your thoughts just entertain you, no matter what they are.

KEY INSIGHTS

Not all thoughts create feelings.

Our thoughts are actually harmless and they are only brought to life, through feelings, when 1. we believe them, or 2. they grab our attention.

When our level of awareness is high (we understand that we are feeling our thinking), we can choose which thoughts to believe.

Do not try to make negative thoughts go away, this is giving them attention, which makes them likely to stay.

Not believing a lousy thought makes it more likely to pass, making space for a new thought to appear.

We are only one new thought away from a new experience (a new feeling).

CHAPTER 4

REALITY HAS NO DESCRIPTION

Some things in life are enjoyable, and some are annoying. Is this true?

We all create descriptions for the people (including ourselves), things and situations in our lives. We do this using adjectives (describing words). For instance, 'my work colleague is *annoying*', or 'that piece of work is a *big* deal', or 'I *love* playing football'.

However, people, things, events or circumstances (reality) have no actual description assigned to them. They are not positive or negative. They are simply 'what is'. The positive or negative feelings are created when our thinking makes-up a description for the person or event and we believe it. The description is not true (objective, unchanging and indisputable).

I can guarantee to you that there is no such thing as a 'big' deal or a 'difficult' situation. Notice how calling it 'big' or 'difficult' often makes it scary, or can make us feel insecure.

So, it is not true that some things are enjoyable, and some are annoying. These are thought created made-up descriptions.

The description might appear true to us, because if we believe it, then it will create real feelings. We do not always choose the description, as we cannot control our thinking all of the time. But when we understand that we do not have to believe the description, then we can start to accept reality just as it is.

KEY INSIGHTS

Reality (whatever is happening right now) has no description.

Positive or negative feelings come from believing the made-up descriptions that we assign to reality.

When we do not believe the description, we can start to accept reality just as it is.

EXERCISE

Draw a straight horizontal line to represent reality over time. Then mark events that have happened in your life on this line and date them. For each event, add a description (adjective) about how you feel about the event. If the description is positive, place it above the event and above the line. If the description is negative, put it below the event and below the line.

As an example, I could mark the month I moved to Sydney, May 2013, and add the description 'exciting' above the line as I viewed this as a positive event in my life. I could mark the month I tore my cartilage in my left knee playing football, November 2006, with 'painful' and 'worried', as I was concerned that I may never play football again, something that I love.

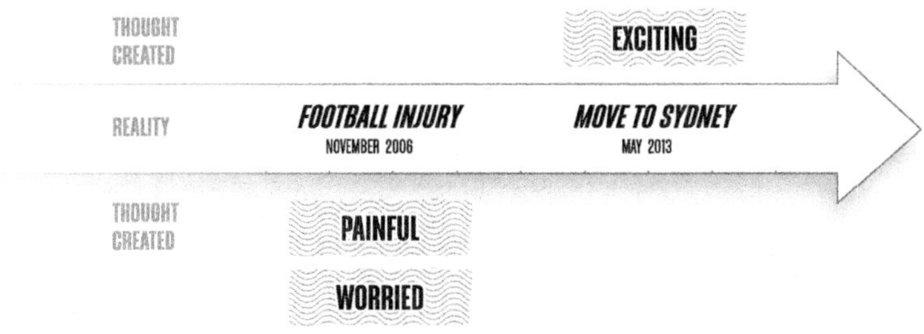

This exercise demonstrates that the events that happen in our life (reality) have no meaning by themselves. They are neutral. But what we do, is give meaning to them by assigning a thought created description to the event, which may be positive, negative or indifferent.

CHAPTER 5

UNIVERSAL TRUTH VERSUS PERSONAL TRUTH

What is the difference between 'universal truth' and 'personal truth'?

As far as I can see, there seem to be *two worlds* operating at the same time. The first is the *external world*. This is the world of *whatever is happening right now*. It is what is happening around us in the present moment and we experience it via our senses. It also includes our feelings in that moment. This external world (without any personal interpretation) may be considered fact or *universal truth*.

The second is the *internal world*. This is the world of *thought*. It is full of subjective stories about ourselves, about others and about the things happening in the external world (past, present or future). This world of thought also includes beliefs (things we hold to be true). When thoughts grab our attention or we agree with them, they are brought to life through feelings. When thoughts turn into feelings, there is a link between the internal and external world, as these feelings are now part of the external world. However, this internal world of thought is made-up. It is full of personal interpretation. It can be considered fiction or *personal truth*.

But what I think may be true sometimes, right?

The only time our thinking is true is when it is giving an accurate, objective account of whatever is happening right now, without any personal interpretation.

We often get universal truth (external world without interpretation) and personal truth (internal world) mixed up. Here are a few ways in which we confuse the two worlds.

As the only moment that actually exists is the present moment, anything that has happened in the past or may happen in the future exists only in thought. So, when we are referring to something in the past or something that may happen in the future, it cannot be a universal truth right now. For example, you may have performed poorly in your exams at high school and therefore believe that you will not perform well in exams in the future. This is a personal truth (if you believe it), not a universal truth, as it involves making assumptions about future events (future exams) based on past performance.

Now you could be giving a factual account of something that happened in the past. For instance, Liverpool Football Club won the Champions League in 2005.

Whilst this may be true about a past event, it does not give us any factual information about the present moment, and it exists only to the extent that it appears in our personal thinking (personal truth).

Sometimes, we believe a thought so strongly that we think it is no longer personal truth and it is, instead, universal truth. For instance, we may believe that constant rain makes everyone feel miserable. This may be true for us (our personal truth), but this does not make it true for everyone (universal truth).

When my clients get confused between personal truth and universal truth, I find that asking the right kind of question often helps them to distinguish between the two.

These are two of the questions I use in these situations: 'Would that still be true if you did not think it?' and 'If nobody had the ability to think, then would that still be true?'

If the answer to these questions is 'yes', then that most likely points to a universal truth. For example, 'The earth is round', or 'gravity exists on our planet', or 'there are three primary colours that make up all colours', are all true right now even if nobody had the ability to think. Whereas, 'I should be treated fairly at work' or 'this book is great!' are personal truths. Without the ability to think they would not be true.

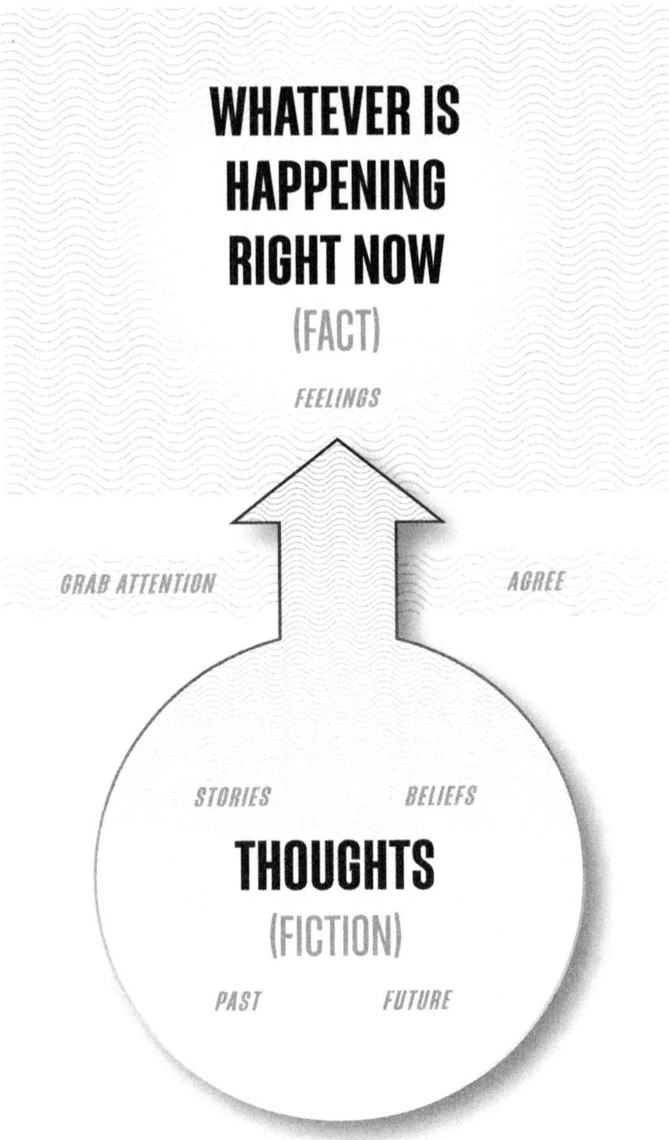
WHATEVER IS HAPPENING RIGHT NOW
(FACT)
FEELINGS
GRAB ATTENTION
AGREE
STORIES
BELIEFS
THOUGHTS
(FICTION)
PAST
FUTURE

Being able to notice when personal truth and universal truth get mixed up has been extremely helpful when navigating my feelings. As we 'wake up' to the fact that the only universal truth is whatever is happening right now, without any personal interpretation, we can start to see the made-up nature of all the personal truths we hold.

KEY INSIGHTS

There are two worlds operating at the same time, external and internal.

The external world of whatever is happening right now (without personal interpretation) can be considered universal truth.

The internal world of thought is made-up and may be considered personal truth.

We often get universal truth and personal truth mixed up. When this happens, a useful question to distinguish between the two is to ask yourself 'would that still be true if you did not think it?'. Answering 'no' points to a personal truth.

CHAPTER 6

THE 'JUDGE' IN OUR HEAD

My first twenty-one years in work were spent in finance as an investment manager. Now that I have switched to a coaching career, I no longer invest money for clients, but I do still invest my own money. And, on the whole, I have been quite successful with my investments.

Yet every time my investment positions move in a loss-making direction, I notice my inner-voice making comments like, 'you should have seen that coming' or, 'why did you make that decision, that was silly?', or 'what if the losses get worse, much worse?'. These judgemental thoughts seem quite strong at times and sometimes I believe them. As a result, I get concerned about my investments and feelings of fear creep in. I start to question my investment skills and even wonder if I should be investing at all.

Where do my negative feelings come from?

We all have a judge in our head that loves to mess with us. He is a master at sabotaging our peace of mind.

He appears through our thoughts (our inner voice) and he relies on us believing these negative thoughts. *Our negative feelings come from believing the judge.*

The judge likes to judge

- Ourselves
- Others
- Events/Circumstances

Your inner voice might be judging what you're wearing, how you look, what you've just done, what you might do, where you are going—the list is endless. It also judges other people—your friends, your family or work colleagues. And it's not just people that get judged. Your inner voice will also comment on events or circumstances, labelling them good or bad.

The judge is not always mean or negative. If it says that you've done a good job, the chances are, you'll experience positive feelings. However, if it says that you have not done so well, that's likely to provoke negative feelings. This might sound obvious, but hopefully you're starting to see that this voice is simply your thoughts making things up. You can't stop the judge from speaking (it will always be there), but you don't have to believe what it says.

If you can learn not to believe your thinking, especially when it is judging, your experience of life will transform in a magical way. You will no longer be constrained by your inner judge's made-up rules. Instead, you will be free to experience life and reality just as it is.

What can I do to help me not believe my judge?

When you notice your judge at work, try saying to yourself something like 'here goes my judge again.' This will help you to take the judgemental thoughts less seriously and separate yourself from your judge.

Giving your judge a name may also help. One of my coaching clients called her judge 'Susan, the cow!'. She told me that it helped her to notice when her judge was in action and made it easier not to believe everything her judge was saying to her. I call my judge 'Mangry' – it helps me to notice when angry Manish is talking to me.

Note, you will normally hear your judge in your primary speaking language and spoken in the same sex as you. For example, I hear a male inner voice speaking to me in English.

Judgement causes so much drama (negative feelings) for us. So:

- Name your judge
- Notice when your judge is talking to you, and
- Don't take it so seriously, it's made-up.

Can I get rid of my judge?

No, you cannot make your judge go away. Your judge will always be with you. My judge talks to me at least once an hour. But understanding that thoughts are made-up enables me to catch my judge in action quickly and not believe what he says.

Later in the book, I will go through a number of ways the judge in our head likes to create drama in our lives. The reason for going through these is to help you to notice when your judge is at work. The instruments that the judge uses include:

- labelling
- comparing
- fear
- a strong attachment to our beliefs
- expectations
- identity/ego
- taking things personally
- making assumptions

Note that these instruments do not always cause drama. For example, it can be helpful to compare, if the purpose is to learn and grow. The important thing is to notice if these instruments are being used to judge, which is not helpful or constructive.

KEY INSIGHTS

We all have a judge in our head.

Our negative feelings come from believing this inner judge.

You cannot make your judge go away, but you don't have to believe it.

Giving your judge a name can help you to notice when it is talking to you and not take it so seriously.

KEY INSIGHTS FROM PART ONE

THE STORY, Of How We Experience Life

Before we move on to look at the kindness of the design of being human, that innate intelligence, happiness and well-being is built-in to all of us, here are some of the key insights from part one:

Our whole experience of life is shaped by our feelings (emotions) from moment to moment.

At all times, we are 'feeling our thinking' in that moment, not our circumstances.

We are experiencing life from the inside-out (via thought), as opposed to the outside-in (via circumstance).

The mind creates lots of different types of thoughts (positive and negative), at a speed of up to one new thought every second.

You cannot control your thoughts all of the time, so trying to become a permanently, or even mostly, positive thinker would be a waste of energy.

We all have negative thoughts from time to time. This is okay and does not mean that there is anything wrong with us.

You cannot change or stop your negative thoughts, but you don't have to believe them.

Your thoughts are a subjective, personal interpretation of events, which can change.

Your thoughts are made-up.

It can be hard not to believe your thoughts, because when you believe them, they turn into feelings, and feelings are real.

Thoughts are harmless by themselves. Thoughts only turn into feelings when they grab our attention or when we agree with them. We all have the power to choose which thoughts to believe.

The descriptions we apply to reality (whatever is happening right now) are made-up by thought.

The only truth is whatever is happening right now (without any personal interpretation). Everything else is made-up by thought.

A useful question to distinguish between universal truth and personal truth (coming from made-up thoughts) is to ask yourself 'would that still be true if you did not think it?' with 'no' as an answer pointing to a personal truth.

Our negative feelings come from believing the judge in our head.

PART TWO

THE BEAUTY

The Kindness of the Design

We carry inside us the wonders
we seek outside us.

Rumi

INTRODUCTION

You only have to watch young children in action to see that we are born happy with a curiosity to explore, learn and play. Yes, kids do cry and become upset when they are hungry, in pain, or don't get what they want. However, they soon move on and return to happiness, as they tend to enjoy what is in front of them at that moment.

This suggests that everything we need to live a fun, peaceful, fulfilling, creative and happy life is built-in to all of us. Our default is happy. The only thing, I repeat, the *only* thing that takes us away from this default is believing our judgemental thinking.

When we get lost and do not feel happy, we all have it within us to find our way back. Our default is peace and contentment. By being fully present and by not taking our thinking so seriously, we can be filled with a deep sense of well-being. It creates a feeling of abundance and vibrancy for life and all the experiences that it will bring, knowing that we will be absolutely fine no matter what. Happiness and well-being are a feeling, and they are always available.

There is nothing that we need to achieve, do, be, or think, to be happy. When we enjoy, or at least accept, whatever is happening right now, we make happiness and love for ourselves and for others unconditional.

Thoughts of scarcity (fear of not having enough)—money, relationships, purpose, knowledge, achievements—which can make us feel unfulfilled are all thoughts that do not have to be believed. For example, we do not have to believe thoughts such as, 'I don't have a purpose', or, 'I haven't achieved enough in my life'. Scarcity is one of the instruments that our inner judge uses to disturb our peace. Knowing that we don't have to believe these thoughts removes the judge's power over us. We all have common sense, wisdom, creativity and instinct—an innate intelligence. These all come through our thinking. When wisdom comes through you, you will feel a sense of ease, a quiet mind, a calmness.

Have you ever had a moment when the solution to a problem suddenly comes to you? Where did that solution come from? It came from your innate intelligence, something that we all possess.

All of this forms the kindness of the design of being human.

CHAPTER 7

TRUSTING YOURSELF

What exactly do you mean when you say 'trust yourself'?

Each of us have been given a beautiful gift—of our body and mind. No matter what you think, you can trust it to do exactly what it needs, when it needs. This is what is meant by 'the kindness of the design'.

Our organs all perform their relevant functions without prompting or direction. If we cut our finger, we can trust our body to heal the cut without intervention. We don't need to think how to heal the finger, our body knows exactly what to do. If we hurt our knee, inflammation protects the knee and acts as a signal that we should rest it.

Now, the mind works in a very similar way to the body. Like 'an inflammation of the mind', lousy feelings seem to be the mind's way of telling us that we are experiencing negative thinking in that moment, and to slow down, rest, leave those thoughts alone and let them pass. As the lousy thoughts pass, our mind tends to quieten, and in this quiet (of the mind), space is made for more inspiring and useful thoughts to enter.

Our minds are extremely powerful. They create thoughts which shape our experience of life. Our minds can be used as a tool for creativity, growth, peak performance, gratitude and fulfilment. Every beautiful piece of art, every amazing invention, every act of kindness has initially come from a thought. We all possess this innate intelligence.

Think of your mind like a pipeline for new thoughts. When the pipeline is open and thought is flowing freely, you will experience a steady flow of new thoughts, insights and creativity. When the pipeline is clogged up with judgemental thoughts, you may experience frustration, staleness and boredom. Quietening the mind *opens up* the pipeline (of thought) by letting the judgemental thoughts pass through.

Trusting yourself is, in essence, another way of saying *let the mind quieten* when it is being judgemental. Then you can observe what fresh new thoughts appear, *knowing that your mind is designed to work in the direction of health and mental well-being*.

When shouldn't I trust my thinking?

If you are experiencing negative feelings, then stop! Do not trust your thinking in that moment. Our negative feelings are warning us away from our thinking in that moment. You see, even negative feelings are part of the kindness of the design and so lousy feelings (coming from lousy thinking) are sending us messages that our wisdom is not working in that moment.

So, if you feel lousy, STOP! Do not trust your thinking in that moment.

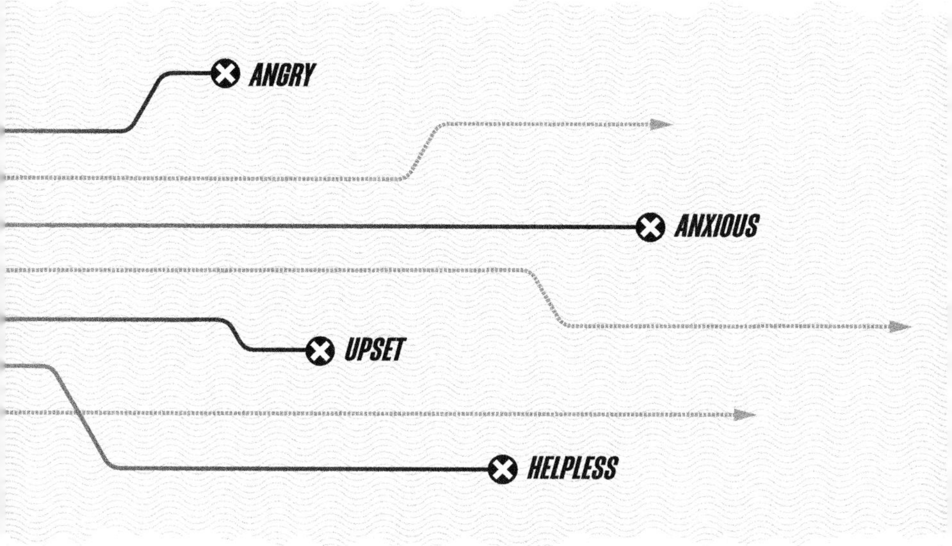

Are positive feelings telling me that my wisdom is talking to me in that moment?

No, positive feelings do not necessarily mean that your wisdom is at work. Positive feelings can come from excitement, innocence, positive judgement (for example, 'you did a good job'), something new, or many other things.

Then how do I know when my wisdom is talking to me?

As your appreciation of your innate intelligence develops, you start to get a feel for when wisdom is coming through you. You are likely to feel a sense of ease, a quiet mind and a calmness when your wisdom is in action. Notice these feelings. Your wisdom might even seem obvious to you (after it has occurred to you); a sense of knowing.

Do not put pressure on yourself attempting to figure out if it is your wisdom, at any moment. Those questions of doubt will most likely bring with them negative feelings, and this is when wisdom is definitely not in action.

KEY INSIGHTS

Our mind and body are designed to work in the direction of health and mental well-being. You can trust it to do this.

We all have common sense, wisdom, creativity and instinct—an innate intelligence.

When your wisdom is in action, you are likely to feel a sense of ease, a quiet mind and a calmness.

If you feel lousy, STOP! Do not trust your (judgemental) thinking in that moment. As you let lousy thoughts pass, the mind will quieten, making space for more inspiring and useful thoughts to enter.

EXERCISE

We all have moments of mental clarity where we know exactly what to do about something or what to say to someone. We cannot predict when these moments will occur. From now on, when you have such moments, notice how you feel. Do you feel calm or anxious? Does the decision about what to do or say seems obvious?

The purpose of this on-going exercise is to help you build your awareness of when your wisdom is talking to you, by noticing how you feel in those moments

CHAPTER 8

HOW TO QUIET THE MIND

What can I do to quieten my mind, especially when I am worked up?

We all get worked up sometimes. It's part of being human. We get into our head and start taking our thinking seriously. Or our thoughts are racing and we get sucked into the scary scenarios we're imagining. In those moments, it can be hard to see the made-up nature of our thinking, but here are some tools and insights that have worked for me, and others, to help you to quiet your mind.

Exercising

I've always exercised regularly, whether that's playing football in the school playground as a child, playing football and squash once a week during my twenties and thirties, or going to the gym and playing tennis in my forties. I've found that when I'm exercising, I am (mostly) out of my head and focused on what I am doing. You simply don't have enough time to think too hard when a football is heading in your direction, or when you're running to reach that tennis ball that dropped just over the net.

Of course, sometimes, I may be mulling something over in my head whilst exercising, perhaps a work problem or a relationship issue. In those moments, I take a deep breath and try to get my head back in the game and, more often than not, this works.

Hobbies

In much the same way as exercising, any pastime or hobby that is absorbing and requires concentration can help quiet the mind. What you do will depend on your personal preferences, but examples include chess, painting, reading and so on.

Getting into nature

Talking a walk and looking at the natural world around us—the sky, grass, trees, flowers and birds is a wonderful way to quiet the mind. When we are absorbed by the beauty of nature, we are often able to get out of our heads and slow our thinking.

Focusing on one of your senses

Applying your full attention to one or more of your senses—sight, hearing, smell, taste and touch—is a powerful way to get out of your head and quieten the mind.

Try intensely focusing on an object in front of you. Apply all your attention to this object. Notice its form, its line and shape. Observe its colour, the depth of colour. Take in everything that you notice about this object. By doing this for a few seconds (thirty seconds, say), you will notice how your mind has slowed down.

You can do the same using your other senses. With hearing, close your eyes and listen intently for a sound far away. Notice the type and magnitude of the sound and then just listen to it without any intention of figuring out what it is. Then switch to a sound nearby and do the same. For taste, really pay attention to the different flavours that you experience as you are chewing food. And with touch, rub your thumb and one of your fingers together. Notice the grooves. Feel the heat as you rub them together. Press a little harder and feel the increased pressure on your thumb and finger.

All of these techniques help to quieten a noisy mind. If, on occasion, they do not work, then try not to be hard on yourself (or the technique), as this would be judgemental and will have the opposite to the desired effect.

Breath focus and meditation

I mentioned before that taking a deep breath when playing sports sometimes helps me to focus and still my mind. Taking a deep breath can help at any time to bring you back to the present. Breath focus can be seen as a way to reset the mind.

Many meditation practices tend to be about focusing on the breath to quieten the mind. Meditation has been around for hundreds of years, across multiple cultures.

When I first began the practice of meditation in my thirties, I must admit, I found it frustrating. My mind would wander and I wasn't able to bring it back to stillness. I thought that meditation did not work for the purpose of quietening the mind. I also thought that with meditation, I could change my thoughts and stop having negative thoughts.

It was only a few years later that I realised that the purpose of meditation is to observe your thoughts, without judgement. With this understanding, I found that meditation (with or without a focus on breath) can help to still the mind.

I now find that I can be in a meditative state (observing my thoughts without judgement) without the actual practice of meditation (that is, sitting still and focusing on my breath). Hopefully, as you begin to see the made-up nature of thought, it will become easier for you to be in this meditative state of mind, more of the time.

Doing nothing to quiet the mind

In his book The Inside Out Revolution, Michael Neill says that 'there's nothing you can do that will quiet the mind faster than doing nothing to quiet the mind'. He uses the analogy of slowing down your car engine. You slow a car engine down by not pressing on the accelerator, so you can slow down your thoughts by 'not revving them up'.

What Michael says here makes a lot of sense to me. When our thoughts are racing and we are feeling lousy, we tend to try and *fix* the situation, as the feelings are uncomfortable. We all have different ways of trying to fix it. I tend to get angry and start shouting (not something that I am proud of). Others may become quiet and inward. The point is that, in these moments of disquiet, we try to do something in the outer world to change our feelings in our inner world. But ironically, if we do nothing in the outer world, chances are that the negative feelings of our inner world will naturally go away as the mind becomes still again.

I understand that it can be hard to not *do something* in the heat of the moment. But consider the possibility that *a quiet mind and a feeling of well-being is our natural state*. Often, we do not need to do anything to return to our natural state.

KEY INSIGHTS

We all get worked up sometimes, it's part of being human.

When our thoughts are racing and we want to quiet or still the mind, we can:

Exercise

Engage in an absorbing hobby

Get into nature

Focus on one or more of our senses

Focus on our breath (with or without the practice of meditation)

Do nothing in the outer world to try and fix the situation or the feelings.

A quiet mind and a feeling of well-being is our natural state.

CHAPTER 9

DEFAULT TO HAPPY

Why do you say that our happiness is built-in?

Imagine a river winding through a beautiful valley. The water in the river is calm most of the time, this is its default state. But sometimes, the weather turns and the water on the surface becomes choppy. The ripples become waves and water seems to be flowing in different directions, almost as if the river is angry. If we are focused on the surface of the river, then, at these times, the river can seem scary. However, no matter how choppy the river is on the surface, if you go deeper into the water it is always calm.

Our thoughts are like this river. A calm or a still mind is our default state. And when our mind is calm, we seem to be content and happy. At times, though, when judgemental thinking is happening, our thoughts become 'choppy'. If we focus on these judgemental thoughts, we start to feel lousy. However, all we have to do at any time is to go deeper (that is, not believe our judgemental thoughts) to notice that a calm mind and contentment is always available. Happy and a calm mind is our default state.

From what I have seen through my own experience and whilst coaching others, is that we are most happy when we are:

- *Fully present* (our full attention is on whatever is happening right now),

  and

- *Non-judgemental* (we do not believe any judgemental thinking that is passing through our mind)

When our mind is quiet, it seems easier to be fully present and non-judgemental. And the reason I say that our happiness is built-in to us at all times, is that both of the above come from inside us and are always available. They have no direct link to our external circumstances.

Yes, short term happiness can be found in external things, such as gifts, clothes, cars, our homes, holidays and so on. From experience, though, happiness from buying, or owning things, or travelling, is usually temporary. Eventually, this kind of happiness wears off, we may become bored of the items and wish for something else. Being fully present as often as possible and being non-judgemental helps to bring lasting happiness.

Our happiness is not linked to what we achieve, do, are or think; it is unconditional. Any conditions for happiness are made-up by our thinking and do not have to be believed.

But for most of us, being fully present and non-judgemental can be difficult. This is understandable, as our judgemental thoughts seem ever present and can be appear very convincing. In the next chapter there are some pointers to help you to return to happiness, when your thinking takes you away from your default state.

KEY INSIGHTS

When our mind is calm or still, we seem to be happy and content. This is our default state.

We are most happy when we are *fully present* (our full attention is on whatever is happening right now) and *non-judgemental* (we do not believe any judgemental thinking passing through our mind).

Being fully present and non-judgemental come from inside us and are always available. This is why our happiness is built-in to us at all times.

Short term happiness can be found in external things, such as gifts, clothes, cars, homes, holidays and so on, but this happiness seems to be temporary. Being fully present and non-judgemental seems to bring lasting happiness.

Our happiness is not linked to what we achieve, do, are or think; it is unconditional. Any conditions for happiness are made-up by our thinking and do not have to be believed.

Being fully present and non-judgemental can be difficult, as our judgemental thoughts seem ever present and can appear very convincing.

CHAPTER 10

FINDING YOUR WAY BACK TO HAPPINESS

NOT TAKING YOUR THINKING SO SERIOUSLY

We all get caught up in fictional stories made-up by our thinking, from time to time. This is okay. It's all part of being human. But when you begin to see the made-up nature of thought, then taking your thinking seriously no longer seems to make sense, especially when you are having judgemental thoughts. The message here is to take your thinking with an element of light-heartedness. After all, it is made-up!

I understand that this seems easier said than done, but the more you practice not taking your thinking so seriously the easier it gets. I say this from personal experience, as well as seeing this with countless clients that I have coached.

ENJOYING, OR AT LEAST ACCEPTING, WHATEVER IS HAPPENING RIGHT NOW

I appreciate that it can be hard to be fully present and apply your complete attention to whatever is happening right now. One thing that seems to help is to surrender to whatever is happening right now, instead of trying to fight it. No matter how much thinking you do and no matter how many times you wish that the circumstances were different, reality is what it is. Fighting with reality, it does not change it. So rather than fighting, it makes sense to enjoy, or at least accept, whatever is happening right now.

How can you possibly enjoy everything that happens?

I agree, you cannot enjoy everything that happens. Some things will be painful. However, continued pain from the same event (what I would call *suffering*) comes from failing to accept *what is* and, instead, believing what happened should not have happened.

Hopefully, to accept what is out of our control sounds obvious, or common sense. However, it's amazing how often we say, either out loud or in our thoughts, that things *should be different* or *we wish they were different*. When we see that it is the *wishing things were different* that is causing our lousy feelings and not the reality in that moment, then we can start to take our wishing thoughts and should thoughts less seriously. We don't have to believe those thoughts!

But if I accept whatever is happening right now won't I become lazy and do nothing?

From what I have observed, people generally do not become lazy when they accept whatever is happening right now. They continue to do things, challenge concepts that seem unfair to them, explore new ideas and are curious to learn. The difference is that they do all of this with an intention to learn, make change, help and have fun. Whatever activity they are doing is no longer a requirement for happiness.

This concept is most obvious, to me, when observing young children. Most children are fully absorbed in and generally seem to accept whatever is happening in the moment. Yet they are not lazy and they have a curiosity to learn and explore, simply because it is fun.

REMOVING CONDITIONS FOR HAPPINESS (unconditional love for yourself and others)

Have you ever heard yourself say (either out loud, or in your head), 'I will be happy when...'? For instance, you may have said (or thought), 'I will be happy when I achieve my goals', or 'I will be happy when I am physically fitter', or 'I will be happy when I am financially secure'.

All of these phrases seem innocent enough, but beware, they are examples of your inner judge trying to make your happiness conditional! They create the illusion that happiness is something that needs to be achieved. Happiness does not need to be achieved, it is built-in to the kindness of the design.

When we see that we do not need to achieve, do, be or think anything in particular to be happy, we make our happiness unconditional. This, in turn, makes our love for ourselves, and for others, unconditional. Noticing when we have set conditions for happiness and choosing not to believe them (they are just thoughts), can help us to return to our default state of happiness.

But I do feel happy when I achieve my goals. Can you explain this?

I'm not denying that the experience of achieving a goal may prompt feelings of happiness. But you may have noticed how this happiness was temporary and faded. This is because your inner judge was most likely commending you for doing a 'good job' by completing the goal (a positive judgement), but once that thought passed, the positive feelings also passed.

What is the problem with the phrase 'I will be happy when...'?

There are two illusions created by our inner judge in the phrase, 'I will be happy when...'.

First, the use of 'when' implies that happiness is something that is attained in the future and not now. This isn't true, happiness can be achieved now by enjoying, or at least accepting, reality just as it is right now.

Second, even when we achieve the goal that we thought our happiness was conditional upon, our inner judge will often change the goal. For instance, we may say that

'I will be happy when I get my dream car'. We may get that dream car and enjoy it for a while, but then our inner judge will create a new goal for us to achieve before we are happy, thereby making our happiness conditional again and something to be achieved in the future.

When you hear yourself say 'I will be happy when...', remember that this is just a thought that you do not have to believe.

KEY INSIGHTS

Try not to take your thinking so seriously (especially when it is being judgemental). After all, your thoughts are made-up!

Enjoy, or at least accept, whatever is happening right now. There's no point fighting with reality, it does not change it.

Some things will be painful, but continued pain from the same event comes from not accepting what is.

People generally do not become lazy when they accept whatever is happening right now. Instead they continue to be curious and explore, simply because it is fun.

Remove any conditions for your happiness, as these are just made-up thoughts created by your inner judge.

CHAPTER 11

GETTING OUT OF OUR HEAD AND INTO OUR LIVES

What do you mean when you say 'getting out of our head and into our lives'?

You may remember the old analogue radios where you had to tune in to a frequency to listen to a particular radio station. Once the frequency was tuned in to the station, the sound would be crystal clear. But when the radio frequency wasn't tuned in to, you would hear a kind of static noise.

This is a great analogy for 'thought'. When our thoughts are tuned in to the frequency of whatever is happening right now, without judgement (what is, right now), then we are 'out of our head and into our lives' and our experience of life seems crystal clear and enjoyable. But when our thoughts are not tuned in to the present moment, then all we hear is noise.

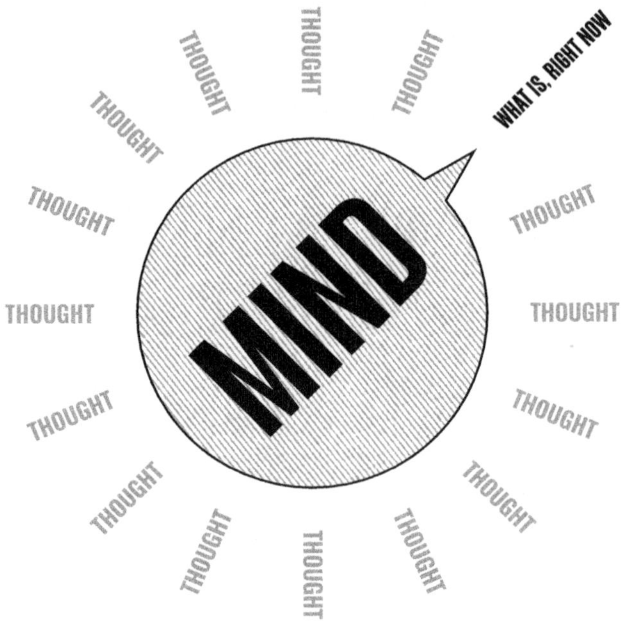

Note that this is simply another way of understanding the concept of being 'present', without judgement. When I'm out of my head and fully present, I get that sense of feeling of being 'in the flow'. Most of us have felt this at times in our lives, but perhaps not as often as we would like. It's when your full attention is on whatever is in front of you right now.

What stops us from being 'present'?

What takes us away from being fully present is our thinking, nothing else.

The past

Our thinking might take us into the past, comparing the present to the past and making a judgement that the past was better. Or our thinking might take us into the past and feel the need to punish ourselves in the present by saying 'I could have made better decisions' (judgement again). This type of thinking is lousy thinking and not helpful. Thoughts about the past take us away from the present moment. Guilt and regret are examples of feelings that signal that we are thinking about and judging the past.

I am not saying that we should ignore our past. Our memory, which is built up from past events, can help us make decisions in the present moment. It is labelling past events as good or bad that's unhelpful and can create negative feelings.

Try thinking of your memory as a bag of supplies that you carry by your side and dip into when needed. You don't want to carry that bag on top of your head and let it weigh you down (with judgement).

The future

Thoughts or worries about the future also take us away from the present moment. Notice when you say to yourself 'what if this...' and 'what if that...', and then start to worry about something that hasn't even happened. All we are doing with 'what if' questions is transporting ourselves away to a made-up world that doesn't exist.

Research from Penn State University showed that 91% of the things that we worry about don't actually happen, and even if they do happen, the outcome is not as bad as we thought. So it doesn't seem like a productive way of spending our time and energy, worrying about what might happen. Planning for the future is useful; worrying about the future is not.

Our beliefs

Even if we're not thinking about the past or worrying about the future we may be comparing the actual reality of the present moment with our expectations or beliefs about reality. For example, if you're looking for a job you might be saying that, given your qualifications, you should have secured a job by now (a belief) and questioning why this hasn't happened yet. Or you might be disappointed that your partner has not washed the dishes when you believed that they would have done this by now (an expectation). Or disappointed that it's raining when the weather report said it would be dry and sunny (again, an expectation).

Comparing reality with our expectations or beliefs in this way happens in our thinking and takes us away from being fully present in the moment. If we can reduce how much we keep fighting with reality, then this will help us to be more present.

How is this useful to me?

Hopefully you're starting to see that we spend a lot of time judging the past, worrying about the future and comparing the present moment to our expectations and beliefs. All of this happens in our thinking and takes us away from fully enjoying the present moment as it is.

So, when you catch yourself up in your head, notice this and ask yourself 'is this useful?'. And then try to apply your full attention to what is in front of you at that moment.

KEY INSIGHTS

When our thoughts are tuned in to whatever is happening right now, without judgement, then we are 'out of our head and into our lives'. This is simply another way of saying being present, without judgement.

The only thing taking us away from being present is our thinking.

We may be focused on the past (our memories) and judging the past is not useful.

Try thinking of your memory as a bag of supplies that you carry by your side and dip into when needed. You don't want to carry that bag on top of your head and let it weigh you down (with judgement).

Planning for the future is useful; worrying about the future is not.

91% of the things that we worry about don't actually happen, and even if they do happen, the outcome is not as bad as we thought.

Notice when you are comparing your current reality to your expectations or your beliefs and ask 'is this useful?'

KEY INSIGHTS FROM PART TWO

THE BEAUTY, The Kindness of the Design

Before we move on to looking at the most common instruments that the judge in our head uses to create lousy feelings, let's recap on the key points from this part:

Our mind and body is designed to work in the direction of health and well-being. You can trust it to do this.

We all have common sense, wisdom, creativity and instinct—an innate intelligence.

When your wisdom is in action, you are likely to feel a sense of ease, a quiet mind and a calmness. Notice these feelings.

If you feel lousy, then STOP! Do not trust your (judgemental) thinking in that moment. As you let the lousy thoughts pass, the mind tends to quieten, making space for more inspiring thoughts to enter.

Ways to quiet the mind include exercise, hobbies, getting into nature, focusing on your senses, breath focus and doing nothing to try and fix the situation or your feelings.

We are most happy when we are fully present and non-judgemental. These are built-in (come from inside us) and are always available.

Happy is our default state. It is not linked to what we achieve, do, are or think. The only thing that takes us away from this default is believing our judgemental thinking.

For most of us, it can be difficult to be fully present and non-judgemental. Some signposts to find our way back to happiness are:

Not taking your thinking so seriously

Enjoying, or at least accepting, whatever is happening right now

Removing conditions for happiness.

We all spend a lot of time in our head, judging the past, worrying about the future and comparing the present moment to our expectations and beliefs. All of this is happening in our thinking and is taking us away from fully enjoying the present moment as it is. Getting out of your head and into your life can greatly enhance your enjoyment of life.

PART THREE

THE DRAMA

Instruments of the Judge

Out beyond ideas of wrongdoing and rightdoing, there is a field. I will meet you there.

Rumi

INTRODUCTION

We have already introduced how the judge in our head creates so much drama (lousy feelings) in our lives. In this part, we will look at a number of instruments the judge often uses to create this drama. The purpose of highlighting these is to help you catch the judge in action quickly and more easily, thereby reducing the amount of time you spend in negative feelings.

Note that the instruments themselves do not cause negative feelings, they can be useful. The important thing is to notice if these instruments are being used in that moment to judge, which is not helpful or constructive. And the easiest way to see if they are being used to judge is to *notice how you feel*. Lousy feelings point to judgemental thinking.

MIND
EGO - LABELS - FEAR - ASSUMPTIONS - COMPARING - TAKING THINGS PERSONALLY - EXPECTATIONS - BELIEFS -

CHAPTER 12

LABELLING

A label is an adjective—good, bad, right, wrong, fun, boring, noisy, smelly, cold and so on—used to describe someone (including ourselves), their (our) behaviour, or a situation. The judge in our head often uses labels to create negative feelings within us.

Remember that reality has no description, so the labels we apply are made-up by our thinking and we do not have to believe them.

What's the problem with using words like 'right' and 'wrong' ('good' and 'bad')?

Using words like 'right' or 'wrong' is a version of labelling. The same applies to 'good' or 'bad'. When we use these words there is usually some form of judgement involved in our thinking.

How do you feel when you label something as wrong or bad? For example, you might hear the judge in your head say 'I'm a bad cook', or 'Steven is wrong for spending so much money on his new car', or 'today was a bad day'. In my experience, when we label something as wrong or bad, it generally creates negative feelings within us.

Judging ourselves using the labels 'wrong' or 'bad' is one of the most common reasons I know for people feeling lousy. How often have you caught yourself thinking something like 'I made a bad decision' or 'I am no good at this' and then felt miserable? You cannot stop yourself from having such thoughts, but remember, you do not have to believe them.

What if someone else does something that I think is wrong. Shouldn't I tell them?

To tell someone they are wrong, is a judgement based on your own point of view. They may have a different perspective and just because they do not agree with you, it does not mean that they are wrong. And, by the same token, it doesn't mean that you are right just because many others agree with you. At this point, you could pause, reflect and recognise that people have the right to have an alternative opinion, before you decide to tell them that they are wrong.

What about when there is a 'right' answer, like the correct answer in mathematics. Is it okay to use right and wrong for that?

Where there is only one outcome, using the words right and wrong seems okay. For example, in mathematics, 2 + 2 = 4 is right and 2 + 2 = 5 is wrong. But with any instance *where there is a choice with the outcome,* then there is not necessarily a right or wrong, there is simply a different point of view.

But aren't some things inherently wrong? Is there a problem with labelling racism as wrong, for example?

You may argue that some things are always right or wrong, even if there is a choice. But here's the thing: when we label racism as wrong, we are likely to create negative feelings within us, yet it does not change the reality that racism exists. We can still do the same things that we might otherwise do to stand up against racism, but why feel lousy or angry (or anything negative) in the process by applying a label with our made-up thinking?

Notice the feelings created by labelling something. If the label creates negative feelings for you, then note that the judge is in action and does not have to be believed or taken so seriously.

I disagree. Something like murder is wrong! How can you say that murder is not wrong?

Yes, murder is wrong. And when it comes to setting laws and rules for things like murder, labels are necessary and useful. It would certainly be hypocritical to say 'it is wrong to label something as wrong'!

But when we label anything, note that we are getting into our heads and out of being fully present. No behaviour or action has an actual 'label' attached to it. Life is not like a supermarket with price tags and labels attached to every behaviour or situation. The label is our personal interpretation, made-up by our personal thinking. Even if the vast majority of people agree with the label attached to a behaviour, like 'murder is wrong', this label is still made-up in each person's individual thought.

In the case of murder, yes, there are real world laws, and committing murder has real world consequences. This is not made-up. The real world laws or labels that exist today form part of the reality of whatever is happening right now. But even real world laws are effectively the made-up rules of society, made-up by the thoughts of law makers. And laws can change.

When it comes to any laws or labels made-up by our personal thinking, these laws or labels can be revisited at any time, by us. Perhaps the simplest way of knowing if a law or label needs to be revisited or taken less seriously is to notice when it creates negative feelings.

For anyone questioning this approach, let me add that in no way does it mean that you are justifying something or more likely to do something, just because you take the labelling of that thing as 'wrong' less seriously!

But surely, we have to judge ourselves if we want to improve?

Think about when kids are learning to walk, typically around the age of one. We don't criticise the young child when they fall over during their attempts to walk. Instead, we praise them and encourage them to try again. We do not say that they did a 'bad' job when they fall down, but we applaud them for their effort. The young child will eventually be walking without judgement and they will have enjoyed the process of learning how to walk. I challenge you to apply this approach to everything that you do. That way, you can enjoy the process of improving (without judgement), as well as the goal.

When clients come to me with the false belief that they must judge themselves to improve, I point out that they have made their happiness conditional on improving, and this often helps them to see how this does not make sense.

How are other kinds of labels a form of judgement?

We all label ourselves, other people, events and circumstances. For example, 'I am an introvert'; 'all boys are annoying'; 'mathematics is hard'; 'rainy days are boring'. To some degree, we have no choice but to label, as it helps to generalise and group the vast amounts of information that life throws at us.

The problem with labelling is that it can distort how we see people, or events, or circumstances, creating bias and potentially leading to some form of judgement. For instance, if you believe that you are an introvert (label), then you may believe that you will be bad at sales (judgement) and sales may be a required part of your work. This can cause feelings of stress. Or if you think that all boys are annoying (label)—a common belief of young girls—then you may not be friendly to a boy that genuinely wants to be friends with you (judgement).

All labels are created by our thinking. By not believing these labels or taking them less seriously, we are more able to accept reality as it is, rather than getting into our head and judging people or events.

Is labelling always a problem?

No, labelling is not always a problem. Labelling has its uses. For example, it would be quite difficult to identify and talk about people if we didn't have names. Or it may be useful to describe the personal characteristics that you are looking for when advertising a job. It is when labelling is used to judge that it creates problems.

KEY INSIGHTS

Labels (such as right, wrong, good and bad) are descriptions applied to reality that are made-up by our thinking and do not have to be believed.

Labelling can be useful (for example, to identify people or when making laws) and is not harmful in itself.

Notice how the label makes you feel, and if you feel lousy, then don't take the label so seriously.

Labelling people and their characteristics can create biases and lead to judgement.

CHAPTER 13

COMPARING

I often make comparisons. Can you explain to me why this may not be useful?

Another powerful instrument our judge likes to use is comparison. We might compare ourselves to others. For example, 'she is smarter than me'. We might compare ourselves today to our past selves. For instance, someone might say, 'I used to be so good at painting and now I'm not'. We might compare our circumstances to those of others. For example, 'we live in the smallest house on the street'. We may also compare events, like 'today's football match was not as exciting as last week's match'.

Whilst comparison might seem harmless, notice how you feel when you are making comparisons. Do you feel happier or more fulfilled? You will often find that making comparisons makes you feel lousy. Yes, of course, if we make a comparison where we believe that we are doing better than someone else (for example, winning a tennis match and thinking that we are the better player), then this may make us feel happy, but this happiness is normally only temporary.

Comparison is frequently used as a form of judgement. By making the comparison, we are ranking ourselves or our circumstances as better or worse than someone or something (judgement). Often, we feel miserable and get lost in our thinking about what we could have done or what we may do in the future. Generally, I find comparisons take us away from the present moment and whatever is happening right now.

As with labelling, comparing is not harmful in itself. You may be comparing to learn and grow. I often observe my opponent's style of play in tennis to see if I can learn anything from them. When writing this book, I compared my style of writing to other authors to understand the different styles of writing. I'm sure you can think of many examples where you have used comparisons to learn and grow. This can be useful.

What can I do when I hear myself comparing?

We tend to make a lot of comparisons. But we can take steps to minimise this. When you catch yourself comparing to judge, you can say, 'I don't have to believe that thought'.

Also, trust yourself to know that you are doing the best that you can in that moment given your circumstances at that time. And you can also ask yourself 'how is this comparison helping me?'.

Not believing judgemental comparisons is unlikely to be easy to begin with. We are unlearning a habit that most of us have become accustomed to over our lifetimes. However, if we are able to recognise comparison as an instrument that's frequently used by our inner judge, that will help us not to take the comparisons so seriously.

KEY INSIGHTS

Notice how you feel when making comparisons. If you feel lousy, then you don't have to believe your thinking in that moment, or take it so seriously

Trust that you are doing the best that you can in that moment, given your circumstances at that time

Ask 'how is this comparison helping me?'

CHAPTER 14

FEAR

Back in my college days, I remember having a huge crush on one of my class mates. At the time, I was quite a shy young boy and despite seeing this girl every day, I couldn't find the courage to tell her how I felt about her. Whenever I came close to telling her, thoughts would pop up in my head like, 'what if she doesn't like you back and rejects you?' or, 'you don't deserve someone as pretty as her.' Sometimes, I would get nervous around her, my heart would start beating faster and my legs would tremble. These fearful thoughts and the feelings they created stopped me from asking her out for over a year. By the time I did ask her, it was approaching the end of our college days and she said that it was too late.

We all feel fear at times, like I did at college with this girl. It's just how the mind works. But here are some things that I have learned about fear that can help you when you are in a fearful state.

What is fear and why do we feel it?

Feeling fear is a very natural and common occurrence for all of us. So, what is fear? It seems to me that fear is generally a feeling that comes from the combination of a thought about a future circumstance, and a belief that *we will not be able to handle it*. For example, we might have an exam approaching, be scared of what might happen if we fail and question whether we can handle the consequences of failure. Or we are going on a date, fear being rejected by the other person and wonder if we can handle the rejection.

As Susan Jeffers, psychologist and author, highlights in her famous book 'Feel the Fear and Do It Anyway', every kind of fear (rejection, failure, change, loss of control, lack of money, loss of loved ones, loneliness etc.) can be summarised as the fear that '*we will not be able to handle it*'.

Isn't feeling fear useful when faced with immediate danger because it triggers a flight or fight response?

Yes, this is true. When we are in immediate physical danger, fear can trigger a flight or fight response which can protect us. This is a useful automatic response to fear that is built-in to us. It is part of the kindness of the design of being human. However, in our modern world, this flight or fight response to physical danger is not required very often. After all, how often do we face real, physical danger?

Most of the fear we experience tends to be more psychological fear, that we will not be able to handle a future circumstance. And believing that 'we will not be able to handle it' is the judge in our head in action again!

By definition, the future has not yet arrived, so the future can only exist in thought. Our psychological fears are created by our thinking. Now, if fear comes from a thought, then the impact of fear can be greatly reduced by remembering that you do not have to believe that fearful thought, it is made-up.

Being fearless is not being without fear, it is about understanding the source of this fearful feeling (which is made-up thoughts).

What can I do when I feel fear?

Just to be clear, I am not saying that fear is not real. We can feel fear through our bodies and that is very real. Fear can bring on physical sensations such as your heart beating very fast, stomach churning, tense muscles or a dry mouth. But the source of this fear is a thought and this thought does not have to be believed.

When I feel fearful, I often say to myself 'I will handle it'. This helps me to deal with the fear knowing that I'll be okay no matter what happens. And the reason I truly believe that I (and you) will handle it, is that the evidence shows that we have handled every situation we have ever come across. Because if you are reading this, then you are still alive!

Sometimes, I think that that I'm not good enough to do something and this makes me anxious.

It seems to me that, when we are in a fearful state, we often say to ourselves that *we are not good enough*. For example, we are not good enough in our studies; we are not good enough at work; we are not good enough parents; we are not good enough to get that job. Do phrases like these sound familiar? We cannot stop these fearful thoughts surfacing, but we can choose to give them very little attention by not believing them.

What else can I do if I am feeling stressed?

Did you know that it is not possible to feel stressed and grateful, at the same time? Stress generally comes from the feeling of inadequacy, that we do not have enough or are not good enough. Whereas gratitude comes from a feeling of abundance, appreciating what we do have, knowing that it is enough or that we can handle our circumstances. This is why being stressed and being grateful are mutually exclusive. Think of it like how you cannot sneeze with your eyes open! The next time you feel stressed, pause for a moment and think about what you are grateful for.

Life can feel like a rollercoaster sometimes, as we go from high feelings to low feelings, with the lows often coming from some kind of fear. Sometimes, we have thoughts of not being good enough: This is just how the mind works. Try not to be so hard on yourself when this thought pops up and you feel low. But as you notice the made-up nature of thoughts more often, including your fearful thoughts, the lows on your rollercoaster of life will most likely not feel as low and you will not stay in that negative state for as long.

KEY INSIGHTS

We all feel fear at times, this is natural and common.

Fear is real, it is a feeling that is sometimes felt through physical sensations.

A flight or fight response to physical danger triggered by fear is useful, but is automatic and built-in to the kindness of the design.

In modern day living, we mostly experience psychological fear, which comes from a thought about the future and a belief that *we will not be able to handle it* or that *we are not good enough*.

Given that psychological fear comes from a thought, the impact of this fear can be greatly reduced by understanding that you do not have to believe that thought, it is made-up.

The evidence is that you have handled every situation that has arisen, so an empowering belief to help deal with fear is 'I will handle it'.

You cannot feel stressed and grateful at the same time so if you are feeling stressed, then think of something that you are grateful for.

CHAPTER 15

HAVING A STRONG ATTACHMENT TO OUR BELIEFS

I once coached a client who suffered from a general sense of anxiety almost all of the time and wanted help dealing with it. We explored what might be causing her anxiety and she shared how she always felt the need to keep busy. Digging deeper revealed how, as a young child, her father had taught her that she 'must always work hard'. Innocently, my client accepted this belief and adopted a work hard approach to everything that she did. She studied hard at school and university, worked hard in her career and constantly kept busy in her home with her husband and two children. However, she struggled to relax. So much so that she felt guilty sitting on the sofa at the end of the day or felt bad taking a break at lunchtime to stop and eat.

After listening to her story, I suggested that she had become so strongly attached to the belief that she should 'always work hard', that it no longer served her well. Sometimes, when we become strongly attached to a belief, we can end up judging ourselves according to that belief and have feelings of guilt (or other lousy feelings) when we do not meet that belief. I suggested that she be kind to herself and make working hard her *preference*, as opposed to something that she must always do.

What are beliefs?

Beliefs are things that we hold to be true. They are the rules we use to govern our lives. We all have beliefs. We may have created them or been taught them by our parents, family, friends, teachers or work colleagues. I must work hard to succeed; siblings should be treated fairly; men and women should get paid equally; I am an extrovert; my partner is selfish—these are all beliefs.

Are beliefs harmful?

Beliefs are not harmful by themselves. In fact, some beliefs can be empowering, such as believing that 'I will handle whatever happens' as we discussed in the chapter about fear. The problem arises when we use our beliefs to judge ourselves, others or events. Beliefs are another powerful instrument used by our inner judge to create drama in our lives.

When we have a *strong attachment to our beliefs*, we may get upset or annoyed if someone else does not obey or agree with our beliefs. But here's the thing. There is no reason why someone else has to agree with your beliefs. These beliefs are yours, not theirs. And where do beliefs exist? They exist in our thinking.

How is someone else supposed to know what you are thinking? Also, does it seem fair to judge someone and believe that they are wrong simply because they do not agree with you?

Have all your beliefs stayed constant throughout your life? My guess is that you no longer believe some of the things you believed at an earlier point in your life. As children, most of us believed that 'Santa Claus was real', but we no longer believe that as we grow older. In my teens and early twenties I believed that 'I will never find love in my life', because the girls I liked didn't seem to like me back. I no longer believe that. The point here is that, if beliefs are not constant, then they cannot be the truth. And if beliefs are not the truth, then you do not have to believe them.

Beliefs are simply rules made-up by our thinking, by which we live and often judge ourselves. As we now know, judgement is the cause of our lousy feelings, so it seems to make sense to *not be so strongly attached to your beliefs*.

Surely, one reason for having beliefs is to enhance your enjoyment of life. When we become strongly attached to our beliefs they start controlling us and our experience of life. Ask yourself '*are you using your beliefs to enhance your experience of life, or are your beliefs controlling you and creating negative feelings?*'.

What can I do about my beliefs that will enhance my life?

I try not be so strongly attached to my beliefs. I like to call my beliefs my preferences. This subtle shift from *beliefs to preferences* helps me to not judge myself or others if my own beliefs are not met. Downgrading beliefs to preferences reduces their control over me and helps me to take them less seriously. Combined with trusting myself, this ensures that my actions are loving most of the time.

Let's take an example. If you have a belief that 'you should be kind' then this seems innocent enough. However, what happens if you behave unkindly one day? The chances are that, if you are strongly attached to this belief, you will judge yourself for not being kind and feel lousy. This is not helpful. Instead, if being kind is your preference, then on the occasions when you are not kind, you will forgive yourself more quickly and not feel lousy for long.

But surely I need beliefs like 'be kind' to ensure that I am loving to people, right?

Thinking that you need rules (beliefs) to make sure that you are kind and loving is simply not true! Being kind and loving is our default. It is how we are born and what brings us most joy and peace. In my experience, it is not possible to be kind and loving all of the time, but when our mind is quiet, this loving state is what we revert back to. Just look at the behaviour of children and you will see their joy and natural instinct to be loving. Trust yourself that you will be kind and loving, even without any rules (beliefs) to judge yourself against. Be kind to yourself and trust that you will be kind to others.

KEY INSIGHTS

Beliefs are things that we hold to be true.

They are rules made-up by our personal thinking.

When we get strongly attached to our beliefs, we can end up using them to judge, thereby creating lousy feelings.

Downgrading your beliefs to *preferences* can help reduce self-judgement, judgement of others and of circumstances.

Beliefs can be useful, but notice how they make you feel at any given moment. If you are feeling lousy, don't take them so seriously.

CHAPTER 16

EXPECTATIONS VERSUS REALITY

In the previous chapter, we talked about how having a strong attachment to your beliefs can create a lot of drama in your life. In a similar way, comparing your expectations to your reality (your current circumstances) can also cause negative feelings. For instance, you may expect to achieve a mark of at least 80% in your maths exam, and instead you attain 70%. Whilst this mark is still very high, you are disappointed given your expectations.

I often find with clients that if their current reality meets their expectations, then they are happy. Whereas if their current reality is lower than their expectations then they seem to be unhappy. With the latter, we discuss the cause of their unhappiness. Is it their current reality? Or is it that their expectations have not been met? This often leads them to see that it is not meeting their expectations that is the root cause of their negative feelings. Once they see this, we can discuss what they can do about this. And the answer is normally they can either raise their reality, by taking some action, or lower their expectations.

Expectations are created by our thinking and, as we now know, you do not have to believe that thinking. Does it make sense to judge ourselves, others or circumstances versus our expectations and then get upset or annoyed if our expectations are not met? I would suggest that this makes no sense at all.

Sometimes I don't realise in that moment that I have expectations. How can I spot my expectations?

Watch out for when you use words like 'should', 'could', or 'wish that'. These words normally imply some sort of judgement or expectation that you are applying to reality. For instance, you may hear in your thoughts, 'my friend should not have said that', or 'I could have seen that problem coming', or 'I should not be scared of that'.

I have often found myself having an internal dialogue saying things like, 'I should've done this', or 'what if things were different'. We all know that there are many things out of our control in life and yet we spend a lot of our time wishing things were different. We are fighting with reality, not accepting what is. Author, Byron Katie, refers to this concept in her book 'Loving What Is' and calls it 'arguing with reality'. She says that 'when we argue with reality, we lose 100% of the time'. It makes more sense to focus on what is in our control and accept what is out of our control. This way, we are spending as little time as possible fighting with reality.

Remember you won't necessarily be able to stop yourself thinking should or could, but you do have the power to see that these thoughts of judgement are not particularly helpful. So, the next time you hear the judge inside your head comparing your expectations to your reality, remember that you can choose not to believe your thinking in that moment.

But, if you want to progress, isn't it important to set goals and not just accept the current situation?

I am not saying don't set goals for the future (expectations for the future if you like), but I am simply saying don't spend your time fighting with your current situation. You can act to achieve your goals without being disappointed with your current reality. If you like, you can call it *progress without judgement during the process.*

I once had a business client who sold computer equipment, who became very frustrated whenever he hadn't achieved his monthly sales target. During coaching sessions, he would spend a great deal of the time complaining about the reasons he had not achieved his target. The reasons included: poor support from his administration team to complete the sale; customers leading him on with no intention of buying; it's holiday season. Despite being a very successful salesman, he would sometimes question his skills as a salesman.

When he did this, I would keep returning to the question 'what's in your control here?'. This question would sometimes annoy him, but he knew intuitively that focusing on what is in his control was more useful than fighting with the reality of things out of his control. And when he focused on what was in his control, he often found ways to achieve his sales target.

KEY INSIGHTS

Comparing your expectations to your reality can result in feeling lousy.

Fighting with reality is not helpful. Instead, focus on what is in your control.

Watch out for words like 'should', 'could', or 'wish that'. They generally point to some form of judgement or expectation.

It can be useful to set goals, but enjoy the progress (without judgement) while you strive to achieve the goals.

CHAPTER 17

LETTING GO OF YOUR IDENTITY (EGO)

What is my identity?

Your identity is often described as 'who you are'. The characteristics that make up 'you'. There are an infinite number of characteristics that could make up your identity and could be defined by you and other people. For example, you may identify yourself as kind, caring, fun, an extrovert, rebellious, careful, adventurous and so on.

Your identity could also be described with what may be considered negative traits, such as selfish, crafty, self-absorbed or lazy. Put together, these characteristics supposedly make up your identity, what you would call, 'I' or 'me' or 'you'.

Yet all of these characteristics are created by and sit in your thoughts (and other people's thoughts). They would not be true if you did not think them. They are not what we would call 'universal truth'.

They are not even static, as your characteristics can change. So, if the characteristics that make up 'you' are created by thought and are made-up, it follows that the concept of 'you' is also thought created and made-up.

Would you still exist even if you didn't use the term 'you'? Your body would exist, you would still be alive, you would still have thoughts and you would still experience feelings. All of these things would still happen even if we didn't label this body as 'me', 'I' or 'you'.

In essence, 'I', 'me' and 'you' are created by our thinking. They are not real, except in our made-up personal thinking.

The concept that 'I' only exists in your thoughts might be difficult to understand or accept, at first. It certainly took me a little while to get my head round it. In order to help see the made-up nature of 'I', consider whether you would be a different person if you had a different name? Your name is just the label that you give yourself and your body. In the same way, the terms 'I' or 'me' are simply labels that we give ourselves, nothing more.

Once you realise that 'I' is simply a label we give ourselves, then you can begin to see the drama we create when our thinking says personalised thoughts like, 'this hurt *me*', or 'why *me*', or '*I* don't like this'. Such thoughts bring negative feelings to this vehicle that we call 'I'.

Imagine, if you can let go of the concept of 'I', then you will no longer feel this personal suffering.

Whatever is happening in any moment is then simply happening, it is not happening 'to me'.

Many texts refer to the concept of 'I' as the 'ego'. When these texts say to drop your ego, what they mean is to let go of the concept of 'I'. Doing this is likely to be much easier when understanding that 'I' or 'ego' is simply something made-up by our thinking. And, once again, you do not have to believe your thinking!

If I am not my identity, then who am I?

'Who am I?' is a question that people have pondered throughout the ages. It's a question that many ask themselves, often numerous times during their lives. Here's my take on it.

'Who am I?' is a question made-up by our thinking that tends to bring with it a feeling of insecurity. If we cannot answer the question, then we think our identity is being challenged or, worse, we have no identity! This can feel like an existential crisis. We then think that we have no stability and no solid place in the world around us. Understandably this seems scary!

Now, it seems to me that, when our mind is quiet and we are thinking with clarity, we tend not to be bothered about answering this question. We are happy just being present.

The judge in our head loves feeding the concept of identity (ego). Without the concept of 'I', the judge would have no-one to hurt. And the question 'who am I?' is simply another device that the judge uses to keep the ego alive. If you see this, then maybe you can let this question 'who am I?' become a passing thought that requires no attention. A more useful question is 'what am I?'. And the answer to this is simple... you are *alive*! That's it. Nothing more, nothing less. Everything that you think about yourself is made-up by your thinking.

A beautiful quote by philosopher Rupert Spira, captures this very concept of letting go of the ego:

In ignorance I am something; In understanding I am nothing; In love I am everything.

KEY INSIGHTS

The characteristics that make up 'you' (your identity) are made-up by thought. They would not be true if you did not think them.

The concepts of 'I', 'me' or 'you' are made-up. They are simply labels applied to your body.

The inner judge likes to keep the concept of 'I' (ego) alive, as without 'I' there is no-one to hurt.

If you can let go of the concept of 'I', then whatever is happening in any moment is simply happening, it is not happening 'to me'.

'Who am I' is not a useful question, and can be treated as a passing thought that requires no attention.

'What am I' is more useful. You are alive! Nothing more, nothing less.

CHAPTER 18

TAKING THINGS PERSONALLY

Imagine that a project has come up at work, which involves tasks that you would really enjoy and believe that you have the right skills for. You speak to your manager and express your interest. However, he tells you that he has already decided to give the project to someone else. You are extremely disappointed and take it personally. You wonder if your manager is questioning your abilities. You are also angry, because you feel that you were not given a fair opportunity. These lousy feelings stay with you for some time.

I am sure you can recall many times when someone has said or done something that you have taken personally, resulting in negative feelings. Taking things personally is another instrument used by your inner judge to create drama.

Why does it not make sense to take anything personally?

Everyone is feeling their own thinking at all times. As a result, everyone is living in their own thought created world most of the time (except when their mind is quiet and they are enjoying whatever is happening in the moment).

Consider this metaphor: Imagine a bubble around every person's head, which holds all of their memories, beliefs and fears. People see and experience everything through this bubble, so their interpretation of everything is distorted by the 'filter' of this bubble. What they see and experience is unique to them and has nothing to do with anyone else. Their world may seem very real to them and they may call it reality, but given that it is thought created, it is made-up.

In his book, *The Four Agreements*, Don Miguel Ruiz talks about not taking anything personally and how this can transform your experience of life. Here is my take on why Don Ruiz's words make so much sense.

People behave in a way that makes sense to them, given what they believe (what is in their bubble). If they say or do something that seems disrespectful to you, it normally has nothing to do with you. It may be because they are in a low state of awareness in that moment. For example, they may be frustrated with something going on in their lives and they take their frustration out on you. It's not personal.

What if someone deliberately means to hurt you and they even admit it?

Even if someone deliberately disrespects you and means to hurt you with their words or actions, you do not have to *take it* personally. There is no direct link between what they do (or say) and how you take it. By taking it personally, you are the one that feels lousy. Also, when you understand that the concept of 'you' is made-up by thought, then you can see that there is no 'you' to hurt. Taking things personally is just another way for the judge in your head to keep the concept of the ego alive and thereby create drama.

I know that not taking things personally can be hard sometimes, but the more you practice this, the less personal drama you will experience.

KEY INSIGHTS

Taking things personally can result in lousy feelings. It is an instrument often used by your inner judge.

People are behaving in a way that makes sense to them, given what they believe. If they say or do something that seems disrespectful to you, it normally has nothing to do with you.

There is no direct link between what someone does (or says) and how you take it.

Not taking things personally can be hard sometimes, but the more you practice this, the less personal drama you will experience

---

CHAPTER 19

MAKING ASSUMPTIONS

We all make assumptions sometimes. Imagine that a person is waiting behind you in a queue to buy coffee. You arrive at the counter and take a few seconds to decide on your order. You hear the person behind you huff, and when you turn around, they appear frustrated. This annoys you. You think that they are really rude and tell them so. The person apologises straight away and tells you that they have just been demoted at work, hence they are really upset and their huff was not aimed at you. You realise that you have made an assumption that the person is being rude to you, but in fact, their behaviour had nothing to do with you.

Making assumptions is another instrument often used by our inner judge to create lousy feelings.

Can you recall a time when you made an assumption about the reason for someone's behaviour and then taken it personally and become upset? We can break this cycle at its source by not making assumptions.

Can I know what someone else is thinking based on their actions?

We often make assumptions about what someone is thinking when they say or do something. We think that we know a person's intentions based on their behaviour. But unless we are mind readers, we cannot know what someone else is thinking!

Surely it would make more sense to simply ask someone what they were thinking and what their intentions were, when they say or do something. We would then get some clarity on their intentions rather than making assumptions. This would save a lot of needless drama.

Yes, someone could lie about their intentions, but surely asking them is better than listening to and believing your own thoughts, as often these will be untrue. Misunderstandings due to assumptions are the source of so many arguments.

I wish others could read my mind and know what I want!

They might not be able to read your mind, but you can help reduce the scope for misunderstandings. Try to be clear with others about your wishes and your needs. Speak up. That way people don't have to assume what you want. Hopefully you can see how not making assumptions and being clear about your preferences can greatly enhance your interaction with others.

Not making assumptions is one of the 'Four Agreements' in Don Miguel Ruiz's book by the same name.

KEY INSIGHTS

Notice when you are making assumptions, as this is another instrument used by your inner judge to create drama.

You cannot know what someone else is thinking based on their actions. Practice asking them what they were thinking and their intentions.

Try to be clear with others about your wishes and your needs, so that they do not have to assume.

CHAPTER 20

SIMPLIFYING THE SOURCES OF NEGATIVE FEELINGS

We have already talked about how all negative feelings come from some form of judgement, which is made-up in our thinking. The most common instruments used by the judge are labels, comparisons, expectations, fear, ego, a strong attachment to our beliefs, taking things personally and making assumptions.

I have tried to simplify these instruments to just two:

1. Fear
2. A strong attachment to our beliefs

I have found this simplification useful, as when I am up in my head and feeling lousy, I ask myself, 'is this a fear or a strong attachment to a belief, or both?'. This helps me to catch my judge in action more quickly.

This simplification works, because labels, comparisons, expectations and the ego are almost a more specific form of a fear and/or a strong attachment to beliefs. For example, if we label a behaviour as right or wrong, then we must be basing this classification on an attachment to a belief. Or if we have an expectation, this too can be linked to a belief. This expectation can also introduce fear (of not meeting the expectation).

Comparisons often give rise to a fear that we are not good enough, or that we should be better (belief).

Whenever you feel lousy, you can ask yourself 'is this a fear or a strong attachment to a belief?' in order to help you identify the source of the negative feeling. Of course, you can also do nothing, knowing that the lousy feeling will pass as your thoughts change naturally.

KEY INSIGHTS FROM PART THREE

THE DRAMA, Instruments of the Judge

Before we move on to seeing how this understanding—that we are feeling our thinking at all times; that thoughts are made-up, so they do not have to be believed—can be applied to everyday situations, here's a recap of some key points about instruments often used by the judge in our head to create drama.

Our inner judge often uses instruments such as labelling, comparisons, fear, a strong attachment to our beliefs, ego ('I'), taking things personally and making assumptions to create drama in our lives.

Becoming aware of these instruments can help you catch your judge in action quickly and more easily, thereby reducing the amount of time you spend in negative feelings.

These instruments are not harmful in themselves, they can be useful. Notice how you feel and if you feel lousy, then the instrument is being used to judge in that moment.

Labelling of people, things, behaviours and events is made-up by thought and can be unhelpful. These include good, bad, right and wrong. Notice what type of feelings are created by the labelling.

Comparing is another instrument often used by the judge. When you find yourself comparing, trust yourself to know that you are doing the best that you can in that moment.

Fear is generally a feeling that comes from a thought about a future circumstance and a belief that *we will not be able to handle it or we are not good enough*. Knowing that fear comes from a made-up thought, that does not have to be believed, can greatly reduce the negative impact of fear.

Having a strong attachment to your beliefs can create judgement and negative feelings. Downgrading your beliefs to *preferences* can reduce the negative impact of beliefs.

Watching out for words like 'should' or 'could' or 'wish that', can help you spot your beliefs and expectations. There is no point fighting with reality. You are better off focusing on what is in your control.

The concept of 'I', 'me' and 'you' is made-up by thought and is often called the 'ego'. Letting go of your ego can reduce a lot of personal drama, as there is no longer a 'you' to hurt.

Try not to take things personally, as this is just another way for the judge in your head to keep the concept of the 'ego' alive.

Avoid making assumptions about what others are thinking, and try to communicate your preferences to avoid misunderstandings.

The instruments often used by the judge to create drama can be simplified to

Fear

A strong attachment to your beliefs

EXERCISE

JUDGE-WORD BINGO

To help you notice how often your inner judge is in play, here's a little game that you can try. I call it 'judge-word bingo'. Below are a number of words used by your judge to create lousy feelings. They are linked to the instruments of the judge that we have discussed in this part of the book. Remember, the words in themselves are harmless, but if they create negative feelings, then the judge is using them in that moment.

Over the course of two days (or a weekend), tick the words off if you say them three times, either out loud or in your thoughts.

Good
Bad
Right
Wrong
Better
Worse
Unfair
Should
Could
Should have
Could have
I am
He/she is
Life is
What if
I need
I don't like

This exercise will help you notice how often your judge is in action!

PART FOUR

THE EXTRAS

Putting It Into Practice

The world is full of magic things patiently waiting for our senses to grow sharper.

W.B. Yeats

INTRODUCTION

So far, we have learned about the mechanics of how we experience life. That is, you are feeling your thinking; thoughts are made-up and do not have to be believed; the only truth is whatever is happening right now; and negative feelings come from believing the judge in your head.

We have also discussed the kindness of the design of being human. That you can trust your body and mind to do what it needs, when it needs. That even negative feelings are part of the kindness of the design, as they are telling you not to trust your thinking in that moment. We have talked about how our default state is happy, and the only thing that takes us away from happiness is our thinking.

And we have looked at a number of instruments used by our inner judge to create lousy feelings.

In this part, we will look at how we can apply what we have learned to a number of topics that clients most commonly come to me for coaching and guidance. I have loosely grouped these topics under two headings:

1. Personal performance
2. Relationships (including the relationship with yourself)

The following chapters will help you see how you can put the theory into practice in everyday situations.

PERSONAL PERFORMANCE

CHAPTER 21

ACHIEVING PEAK PERFORMANCE

How can I perform to the best of my abilities?

In an ideal world we would all be performing to the best of our ability at all times in whatever we do. In reality, this does not seem to happen. For example, I sometimes allocate time to complete a piece of work, sit down and have all the necessary resources, yet I struggle to concentrate and my mind feels blocked.

I once coached a semi-professional tennis player who could not understand why, on some days, he simply could not hit the ball as well as he knew he could. He claimed that, at these times, his technique was unchanged and his effort was consistent, however the shots were not going where he wanted them to go. I'm sure that everyone has similar stories of not achieving peak performance at times.

Through personal experience and from my years of coaching, the primary reason for not achieving peak performance is because we get into our heads and out of the task at hand. There are many reasons that we may be in our heads. We may be distracted by thoughts of something else, like another piece of work, or what's for dinner! We may be frustrated with our performance and judging ourselves, because we think that we can do better! Or we may be ruminating about our past performance, like in the case of my tennis playing client, who may have been thinking about the last shot that he played.

When we are up in our head, it is more difficult to pay full attention to what is in front of us right now. Something which I share with clients is a simple formula for peak performance:

Peak performance = capacity - noise

'Capacity' refers to your natural ability, skillset and effort applied, and 'noise' is how much thinking is going on.

When we are operating at peak performance there is not much *thinking* happening. We are simply *doing* based on our capacity at that time. People often refer to this as being 'in the flow'.

How can I be 'in the flow' more of the time?

The answer to this is to quiet the mind. Earlier, I suggested different ways to quiet the mind such as exercising, breathing and focusing on your senses. I also talked about doing nothing to quiet the mind, because a quiet mind is our natural state. Any or all of these techniques can work at different times.

From what I've observed, the people that are best at being in the flow, more of the time, are those that recognise the made-up nature of thought and don't take their thinking so seriously.

KEY INSIGHTS

Peak performance = capacity – noise, where 'capacity' refers to your natural ability, skillset and effort applied, and 'noise' is how much thinking is going on.

Being 'in the flow' is easier when you recognise the made-up nature of thought and don't take it so seriously, resulting in a quiet mind.

CHAPTER 22

UNDERSTANDING WHAT IS 'YOUR BEST'

'Just do your best'. This is a phrase that I heard throughout my schooling years and often at work too. It was something that others would say to me, but also something that I would say to myself. 'Just do your best' might sound like an innocent statement, but I often felt lousy when I believed that I hadn't done my best.

As the years have passed, I now realise that 'you have not done your best' is simply my inner judge talking to me and I do not have to believe that thought.

What is 'your best'?

'Best' is something made-up by your thinking (or someone else's thinking). Best is a comparison, perhaps to something that we think we should be able to do (an expectation) or a comparison to someone else. We discussed earlier how comparisons may not be helpful so asking yourself 'is this your best?' is often an unhelpful comparison. Notice how it makes you feel.

Remember the example of the baby learning to walk. It shows you that you do not need to keep asking 'is this my best?' in order to make progress. Instead, why not recognise that you are always doing your best in that moment based on your knowledge, experience, skills and circumstances in that moment? Your best may change from moment to moment and that's okay. By doing this you will minimise the self-judgement that comes from asking 'are you doing your best?'.

KEY INSIGHTS

'Your best' is a made-up comparison coming from thought that does not have to be believed.

Trust yourself that you are always doing your best in that moment based on your knowledge, experience, skills and circumstances in that moment.

This will reduce the self-judgement that comes from asking 'are you doing your best?'

CHAPTER 23

MAKING DECISIONS

Sometimes, I struggle to make decisions and this makes me anxious. What can I do in such situations?

A few years ago, my niece, who was then at high school, asked me to help her decide which college to choose. She had narrowed it down to two colleges, but was struggling to come to a final decision. She had written down the positives and negatives of each college, but that made her more indecisive and confused. This manifested as feelings of anxiety and stress.

Given that she felt so stuck in her decision-making process, I suggested that she grab a coin and play a little game. I asked her to assign one college to heads and the other college to tails and then to toss the coin. As the coin landed, I asked if her immediate reaction to the result was joy or disappointment. She was pleased, and I told her that this immediate reaction is likely to give her a clue as to which college she really wants to choose. I went on to explain that this simple game was attempting to by-pass the rational, intellectual mind, and tap into her inner knowing. I explained to her that she can trust her decision-making when she is feeling calm.

We often get stuck when making decisions, because we think that there is a right and wrong decision. And this judgement (of right and wrong) makes us anxious and scared to decide. Judgmental thoughts block the pipeline of clear thinking and make it difficult for our inner wisdom to come through us.

Now imagine how it would feel if you could drop the belief that there is a right and wrong decision. After all, right and wrong are labels, made-up by our thinking, which do not have to be believed. By dropping this belief, you will find it easier to make decisions. It takes the stress out of decision making, which in turn can reduce anxiety.

You see, when it comes to making decisions, you either *know* what decision to make (your inner guidance is telling you) and trust yourself in such instances, or you do not know what decision to make. But in these instances, you could literally toss a coin or roll dice to decide, knowing that if there are no right or wrong decisions (except in your made-up thinking), then you will be absolutely fine no matter what. Remember, your happiness is not conditional on you achieving, doing or being anything (only your made-up thinking tells you this).

Of course, we can all look back at decisions that we have made in the past and judge them as right or wrong given the outcome, but try to remember that, at all times, we are doing our best based on the information available at the time. Judging a decision after the event is not helpful, unless this is done to learn for future decision making.

KEY INSIGHTS

When making decisions, we often get stuck, because we think that there is a right and wrong decision.

Judgmental thoughts (of right and wrong) block the pipeline of clear thinking and make it difficult for our inner wisdom to come through us.

You either know what decision to make (your inner guidance is telling you) and trust yourself at such times, or

You do not know what decision to make. In these instances, you could toss a coin or roll dice, knowing that you will be absolutely fine no matter what, as your happiness is not conditional on this (or any) decision.

CHAPTER 24

FEELING EMPOWERED

Clients sometimes come to me with feelings of frustration, anger or upset about their situation and a sense that they can do nothing about it. They may feel like a victim of their circumstances and use phrases like, 'the universe is conspiring against me', or 'why am I so unlucky'. I once coached a client who was looking for a new job, but was frustrated that he was not getting interviews. He had many victim-minded stories running through his head about the reasons for the lack of interviews, such as, 'it must be my age', and, 'I must have done something bad in my past life to be this unlucky'. He was struggling to accept the reality of what was happening in that moment. This resulted in him feeling disempowered and hopeless.

We all face situations which are out of our control, where we do not like the outcome. This is just a part of life. However, how we feel and how empowered we feel in those situations, will depend on whether or not we believe the victim-minded thoughts and the subsequent actions that we take.

Here are some things that you can do to feel more empowered and feel less like a victim of your circumstances.

FOCUS ON WHAT IS IN YOUR CONTROL

The ancient Stoics say that 'the happiest people are those that do not worry about what is out of their control'. What is the point of focusing on what is out of your control? You cannot change it and you are likely to feel helpless as you may want a particular outcome, but know that you cannot do anything about it. Surely you are better off accepting what you cannot control and instead focusing on what you can?

Focusing on what is in your control sounds so obvious, and yet we often forget to do this. I have to remind myself to do this a number of times daily.

I can't tell you why our thinking likes to focus on what we cannot control. Perhaps our inner judge likes making us feel miserable or perhaps we feel comfort knowing that something is out of our control and therefore it is not our fault. Whatever the reason, it is much more helpful to face what is in front of us and ask what is in our control.

And remember, even if you cannot control the circumstance, you don't have to believe any lousy thinking about it.

If this is the only thing you take away from this book, this could change your life for the better. It certainly has for me.

THREE TYPES OF BUSINESS

One approach that I have found particularly helpful to feel empowered is to categorise circumstances into three different types. This is something that Byron Katie does in her book 'Loving What Is'. She describes them as: 'my' business—what you think, say and do; 'your' business—what others think, say and do; and 'events or circumstances' (Katie refers to this as 'God's' business)—things out of any person's control (the weather, for example).

She says that the only business in your control is 'my' business, so try and spend as much time as you can in 'my' business. This is simply another way of saying 'focus on what is in your control'. We cannot control what other people think, say and do, it is their business. So, try to stay out of other people's business and remember, don't take it personally.

Throughout our lives, we will encounter events or circumstances which are out of our control—the weather, changes in our health, changes in property prices, job opportunities, train delays, what questions come up in our exams and so on. Our choice, again, is to either accept these events and circumstances as they are, or to fight with reality in the hope that they were different (and never winning this argument).

What about when you are doing an activity with someone else?

Of course, there will be times when 'my' business and

'your' business overlap like when you are doing things together. On these occasions, if you cannot agree on what to do, then try and communicate your preferences as clearly as possible and attempt to reach a middle ground. If this is not possible, then one of you may have to compromise. And that is okay. Importantly, if you are the one compromising, then try to do it without resentment and accept what is now out of your control.

What if my manager doesn't think highly of me? Isn't that 'my' business?

Another example of 'my' business and 'your' business potentially overlapping is if your manager says negative things about your work. They may not think highly of you and this could impact your chances of promotion. With this, you may argue that the impression that your manager has of you is now 'my' business. Whilst you might be able to influence what your boss thinks of you, you cannot control their thinking. This is their business and you have a choice of either accepting it or feeling frustrated by it.

By spending as much time as possible in 'my' business (what's in your control), you are likely to feel less helpless and more empowered.

B.E.D. TIME STORIES

No, I'm not talking about stories that we read to children to try and get them to sleep! B.E.D. is an acronym for Blame, Excuse and Denial. These are three things that we often do that are not helpful in enhancing our experience of life. Whilst we might feel justified in using these terms in a particular situation, by doing so, we can feel powerless and like the victim. Neither of these is going to make us feel particularly great.

Instead, by taking ownership of the situation and by being accountable for our behaviour, which is in our control, the power and responsibility comes back to us.

Have you found yourself blaming someone else for the situation that you're in or how you are feeling? Have you made excuses for not getting something important done? Have you avoided a difficult conversation with someone because you didn't want to deal with the consequences? All of these things could be justified, but telling ourselves B.E.D. time stories is going to make our story of life less fun.

Remember we are constantly feeling our thinking, so victim-minded thinking is likely to make us feel lousy. Whereas, taking ownership and asking what's in our control, is going to make us feel empowered.

KEY INSIGHTS

We all face situations which are out of our control where we do not like the outcome. Focusing on them can make us feel disempowered and like a victim. This is not helpful.

Instead try to bring your focus back to things that are in your control, and accept the things that you cannot control.

You don't have to believe any lousy thinking about your circumstances.

Try to focus on 'my' business, not 'your' business or 'events and circumstances'.

Watch out for when you are in a 'blame', 'excuses' and 'denial' (B.E.D. time stories), frame of mind. Instead take ownership of the situation and be accountable for your behaviour.

CHAPTER 25

LESS 'WORK', MORE 'PLAY'

What can I do to make work more enjoyable?

When my daughter's friends come over for a play date, I tell them that there is only one rule in this house, and that is to 'have fun'. Surely it makes sense to aim to have fun in whatever we are doing, be it during work, school or leisure. Yes, it may be harder to have fun when we are doing something that we don't particularly enjoy or that feels like work. And it's not possible to have fun all of the time, but it seems to me that setting a goal of having fun is a pretty good one.

Some believe that in order to take responsibility, you must take things seriously and not have as much fun. However, taking responsibility and having fun are not mutually exclusive. You can do both!

Being grateful for whatever work you are doing in that moment can also make that activity more enjoyable. If I'm doing something that I don't particularly enjoy, such as cleaning the house or doing paperwork, then instead of saying I've 'got to' do this, I say I 'get to' do this. With this subtle change of words, I appreciate what I get to do. For example, when cleaning the house, I appreciate that I have a house, which makes cleaning it more enjoyable. When completing paperwork, I think that I'm lucky that I have things that require paperwork to be completed. Saying 'I get to do' the activity seems to change my experience in a positive way.

Have you noticed that when you call something 'work', it doesn't seem as enjoyable, but when you call something 'play' it seems far more fun. The truth is that no activity is work and no activity is play. The words 'work' and 'play' are simply adjectives that we use to describe an activity. The activity itself is neither. The concepts of work and play exist only in our thinking and remember that you do not have to believe your thinking. Imagine how it would feel if you considered everything to be 'play'. Chances are that you will enjoy yourself far more of the time if you are just playing.

Children are particularly good at thinking that everything is play. Have you noticed that young children like pretending to be an adult and 'work' activities for them are simply 'play'. They might pretend to be a firefighter, or a doctor, or an office worker. They may imitate cleaning the house with a toy vacuum cleaner, and all of this is just fun for them. You see, children don't start labelling activities as work or play, they simply *do* and make the most of what they are doing. Labelling activities as 'work' does not seem to enhance our enjoyment of it, so why label it?

I'm not suggesting that we should be in denial about what we enjoy and what we don't enjoy. But why make an activity even less enjoyable by calling it work? We are always feeling our thinking. So, if we are thinking that something is work then we probably won't feel as good in that moment. Calling it play is likely to feel much better.

KEY INSIGHTS

Aim to have fun whatever you are doing, be it during work, school or leisure.

Taking responsibility and having fun are not mutually exclusive, you can do both.

Being grateful can make any activity more enjoyable. Try saying 'I get to' do this, instead of 'I got to' do this.

Notice how you feel when you call something 'work'. Instead, you could call it 'play', at the same time remembering that 'work' and 'play' are made-up thoughts that do not have to be believed.

CHAPTER 26

BOREDOM

I sometimes get bored. Why is this?

Here is a perspective on boredom:

You get bored when your thoughts are moving faster than your reality.

For example, you might be at work, but you are day-dreaming about what you want to do after work. Or you're at school in a maths class wondering what the point of learning how to divide fractions is when you're never going to use this. When you are bored, your thinking is taking you away from the reality of the present moment.

Next time you're bored try pressing the soles of your feet firmly into the ground. This will help you to slow down your thinking and bring you back to the present moment.

Another tip when you are bored and your thinking is racing, is to ask yourself 'what will my next thought be?'. Amazingly, when you ask yourself this question your thinking stops momentarily and breaks up wherever your train of thought was taking you. This can work for any lousy thinking.

KEY INSIGHTS

Boredom is when your thoughts are moving faster than your reality.

When you are bored, try to bring yourself back to the present moment.

Asking yourself 'what will my next thought be?' can break up your current train of thought.

CHAPTER 27

THAT'S UNFAIR

I get upset when someone or something isn't fair to me. Surely, it is reasonable to expect fairness, right?

Most of us hold a belief that life should be fair. For example, you might believe that you should be treated fairly and equally at work regardless of your race, sex, age or background. You might believe that your parents should treat all their kids fairly. You might believe that if you put in the hard work for a project then you will reap the rewards. You might believe that you and your partner should do an equal amount of housework.

It might seem reasonable to assume that you should be treated fairly. However, this is just a belief that many of us hold and it does not make it true or the reality. In fact, holding on to this belief often creates negative feelings when reality is not fair to you. There is no point fighting with reality, even if it is not fair. We are better off accepting it.

In other words, try to not be so strongly attached to the belief that 'people or circumstances should be fair'. Making it your preference is fine. However, a strong attachment to this belief only brings with it negative feelings, as you compare the reality to your expectations of fairness.

'Expecting fairness' is getting a special mention in this section on personal performance, as I have found that many clients get stuck in this belief and it hinders their performance levels.

KEY INSIGHTS

Expecting fairness is a made-up belief.

Being strongly attached to this belief can hinder performance levels.

Try, instead, to make 'expecting fairness' your preference.

CHAPTER 28

PASSION IS A FEELING NOT A THING

I'm not sure what I'm passionate about. How can I find my passions?

'What are you passionate about?' I'm sure most of us have been asked this question at some point in our lives. I used to think that passion was a *thing* that excites you. For me, I thought that I was passionate about playing football, or tennis, or solving maths problems (that's the geek in me!). I can recall the ecstatic feeling of smashing the football into the corner of the goal, or hitting a winning shot in tennis when my opponent is at the net. I used to think that my passion was the act of playing football or tennis.

However, I've come to realise that passion comes from the feeling of being 'in the zone' and not thinking about anything else in that moment. In other words, I am passionate when I am fully present. I can even get this 'in the zone' feeling when doing other activities that I wouldn't class as my passion. For example, I have felt this whilst vacuuming my flat, listening to loud music blasting out (admittedly, not every time). I have also felt this when I'm fully engaged in a conversation with someone.

Now I think of passion as a feeling of being in the zone no matter what you are doing. In other words, *passion is giving your full attention to what is in front of you right now*.

Hopefully, this will take a significant weight off your shoulders, knowing that passion is not a thing and you do not have to find it. You simply have to be present and the wonderful feelings associated with passion can ignite in that moment.

KEY INSIGHTS

Passion is a feeling and not a thing.

Passion is giving your full attention to what is in front of you right now and this can be applied to any activity.

RELATIONSHIPS

CHAPTER 29

ACCEPTANCE AND COMMUNICATION MAKE FOR HEALTHY RELATIONSHIPS

What can I do to improve my relationships with others?

From my experience, two of the key components of a healthy relationship with your partner, your parents, your child, work colleagues, a friend or family members, are full acceptance of the other person for who they are (without judgement) and open communication, especially when you disagree on something.

Acceptance

We cannot fix or change anyone, they can only fix or change themselves. When we understand this, then it makes sense to accept them for who they are, exactly how they are. We all have growth to do and that will, no doubt, happen at a different pace for everyone. It does not seem fair to judge someone based on our beliefs. After all, no one likes to be judged, so why judge others?

If we can accept someone without judgement, then how we see what they say and do is likely to change in a positive way. We are spending more time in our own business as opposed to the other person's business.

I understand that this might be a tough ask, especially when you care about this person, or they might live with you. But surely, caring about them means respecting them and in turn, this means accepting them.

No two people are going to have exactly the same beliefs. Beliefs are made up in our thinking and one person's beliefs are no more right or wrong than another's. Beliefs are just a point of view. Everyone has a right to have their own point of view, and acceptance involves respecting this.

There is a beautiful quote that I once read about acceptance, without expecting anything in return. It goes like this:

Even after all this time the Sun never says to the Earth 'you owe me'. Look what happens with a love like that, it lights the whole sky.

Communication

Another key component of a healthy relationship is communication. We have already said that two people cannot have exactly the same point of view on everything so when two people disagree, the key is to talk to each other. If you cannot do what you want to, because someone else disagrees, it makes sense to talk to see if there is a middle ground. Also, by communicating, you can find out how important this issue is to them. You may choose to compromise when you find out that something is really important to the other person or vice versa.

With communication you avoid the danger of making assumptions about what the other person thinks or how important this is to them. By talking and genuinely listening, you are also showing respect to the other person that their opinion and what they want matters. You're unlikely to get what you want every time. But hopefully you're okay with that, because you recognise that when more than one person is involved you're showing love and care for the other person by listening to their wants.

KEY INSIGHTS

We cannot fix or change anyone, they can only do this themselves.

Try to accept others without judgement, exactly as they are.

Communicate clearly, to avoid the danger of making assumptions.

When you disagree with someone, see if you can find a middle ground.

CHAPTER 30

THREE LEVELS OF COMMUNICATION WITH OTHERS

How can I improve my communication skills?

From what I have observed over the course of my life, communication with other people is often the cause of much drama. To help reduce this drama, consider three levels to listen and communicate:

Level One - Understanding
Level Two - Agreement/Disagreement
Level Three - Judgement

Level one - Understanding

At this level, you are listening with an open mind, hearing what the other person is saying without your thinking getting in the way. You are trying to understand their perspective. Listening to understand is a great way to communicate, as the other person will feel really heard and appreciated.

Level two - Agreement/Disagreement

At this level, you are deciding whether you agree with the other person's point of view. It's okay if you disagree, as you have a right to believe whatever you want. Listening to agree/disagree is also fine when communicating. Perhaps you might even change your mind after listening to the other person's point of view.

If you disagree with someone, a respectful way to tell them may be something like, 'I respect your point of view, but I disagree…', or 'my experience is…', or 'as I see it…'.

At times, it may not be necessary to explicitly say that you disagree. Many conversations flow naturally with each person expressing their viewpoints as part of a discussion.

Level three - Judgement

At this level, you are deciding if the other person's perspective is right or wrong. This is the level at which we get ourselves into trouble and cause drama. By trying to label their perspective as right or wrong, we are effectively telling them that we do not respect their point of view. Who are we to judge who is right and who is wrong? Listening with judgement is not okay! As we now know, judgement can bring us negative feelings. Judgement of others can also trigger negative feelings for them.

Try to avoid judging when communicating with others. Instead, listen with an intention to understand and perhaps agree/disagree respectfully. Of course, it's okay to have beliefs, but the purpose of beliefs and discussing them with others is to engage in conversation, not to impose your beliefs on others, or to prove your point.

See how it feels for you to engage in conversations at levels one and two (understanding and agreement/disagreement) and try not to move onto level three (judgement). I have personally found this very helpful.

KEY INSIGHTS

Listening to understand a person's perspective, without your thinking getting in the way, is a great way to communicate and can help them to feel heard and appreciated.

Listening to agree/disagree is also okay, as you have a right to have your own point of view. Express any disagreement respectfully.

Listening to judge (right or wrong) can create drama and can be disrespectful.

The purpose of beliefs and discussing them with others is to engage in conversation, not to impose your beliefs, or to prove your point.

CHAPTER 31

MONEY AND YOUR RELATIONSHIP WITH IT

I often get anxious when I think about money and whether or not I have enough. How can understanding how the mind works help me to deal with this?

The word 'money' can bring up very different feelings for people. If you have lots of money, then you may feel secure and you may feel happy with a sense of well-being. If you don't have much money, then this may bring up feelings of anxiety, concern that you do not have enough to provide for yourself and your family and worries about how you will survive financially later in life.

Let's consider if these feelings about money actually come from the amount of money someone has, or if the feelings come from something else. I've met some very rich people in my life, with assets over £100 million. I have also met individuals with very little money, who rely on their salary from month to month to pay their bills and put food on the table. What I've observed is that their sense of security about having enough money and their general well-being are not necessarily based on a particular size of bank balance. Some people with over £100 million still worry that this is not enough, or that they might lose it. Whereas some people living on their monthly salary with no savings, are not concerned.

This seems to imply that the size of your bank balance does not necessarily determine how secure you feel about money. Instead, it suggests your thinking about 'how much money is enough' determines whether or not you feel secure. In other words, a feeling of abundance or scarcity (of money) comes from your beliefs about how much is enough, and from fears of losing what you have.

The truth is that money is simply a piece of paper. Globally we have an agreement (faith) that this paper has a value that can be used for exchanging goods and services. Instead of paper, money could have been in the form of gold, or chairs, or screwdrivers! As long as there is an agreement that these things have a certain value, they can be used for exchange. Money, in whatever form we have agreed (coins, notes, bitcoin) is a practical tool for exchanging goods and services.

When we see money simply as a practical tool for exchanging goods and services, we start to see that money in itself cannot buy other things like security, happiness or well-being. It cannot bring a sense of abundance without also *thinking* that it is enough. Security and the amount of money you have are not necessarily linked to each other. If you see this, then your relationship with money will change. Making money can become more fun knowing that it is merely a practical tool and not the source of your well-being.

Try not to confuse money with oxygen. We need oxygen to live every day, we don't need money in the same way.

What is the best way of making money?

Generally, the best way of making money is to make a difference. When you can make a difference for someone or a company, then they are likely to be happy to exchange your services or goods for money. For example, if you are a cleaner and clean someone's house well, then they will happily pay you for it as it saves them time and effort.

KEY INSIGHTS

A feeling of abundance or scarcity of money, comes from your thinking about how much is enough, and your fears of losing what you have, not directly from how much money you have.

Money is a practical tool for exchanging goods and services, it cannot in itself buy security, happiness or well-being.

The best way of making money is to make a difference.

EXERCISE

Here's a little exercise for you. Make a list of the things that you want right now. For example, it might be some new items of clothing, a new vacuum cleaner or a new car. Or it might be greater freedom to choose what you do every day, or security, or more variety in your daily activities. Then, for each of these things, mark down whether or not you can physically buy it. The purpose of this exercise is to help you see what money can and cannot buy (you cannot physically buy freedom and security). Hopefully this will help you see its purpose, remembering that feelings (such as freedom and security) come from your thinking and not directly from your circumstances (how much money you have).

CHAPTER 32

VULNERABILITY AND COURAGE (ARE THE SAME)

When it comes to your relationship with yourself, I frequently have clients coming to me with a belief that being vulnerable is a sign of weakness. They feel the need to put on a positive 'mask' in front of others, even if they are scared. This can result in feelings of loneliness and inauthenticity, as they do not feel understood by others or able to be honest.

I too have been guilty of this, on occasion. Recently, my mother was diagnosed with a serious illness and when informing my partner that same day, I acted positive saying that I was okay. But as it turns out, I was still processing the news about my mother and I was not okay. Later that day, I snapped at my partner about something trivial and unrelated. This resulted in a heated argument that could have been avoided, if I had been willing to show my vulnerability, as my partner would have shown compassion when I snapped at her.

So let's consider if vulnerability is actually a sign of weakness.

I find it difficult to stay strong all of the time. Is this a problem?

Has anyone ever told you to be strong? Perhaps you or someone you love is not well and friends and family tell you to stay strong, everything will be okay. Or perhaps you are struggling financially and people are telling you to have faith, that it will be okay.

Staying strong and positive all the time is impossible, I recommend that you don't even bother to try. Remember we cannot control our thoughts, so our thoughts are likely to create scenarios which seem scary. How are you supposed to stay strong when what you see is something scary?

But isn't being vulnerable a sign of weakness?

No, it's okay to be vulnerable and to say that you are scared. Society often claims that you should stay positive and strong. But as a result, saying that you are scared and showing your vulnerability is often considered a sign of weakness. This is not true! Being vulnerable and expressing your emotions is not weakness, it is the exact opposite. You are expressing yourself authentically without fear of what others think of you.

Brene Brown, a famous research professor and author, has a great definition for vulnerability and courage. It is the same definition for both, which is '*stepping into the arena of life where you cannot control the outcome'.*

For example, would you consider a person who runs into a house on fire in order to save someone, as courageous? Most people would say yes. Would you also say that it is okay for this person, if asked, to say that they are really scared? Again, I suspect the answer for most is yes. This person is vulnerable and courageous at the same time because vulnerability and courage are the same thing.

The message here is that it's okay to be vulnerable and say so. It is not a sign of weakness. In fact, it shows great courage.

KEY INSIGHTS

It is impossible to stay strong all of the time, as fearful thoughts can create scary feelings.

Being vulnerable is not a sign of weakness, it's okay to say you are scared.

Vulnerability and courage are the same, defined as 'stepping into the arena of life where you cannot control the outcome'.

CHAPTER 33

'LOVE' (MY DEFINITION)

I don't think that I have seen a universally agreed definition of 'love'. So I ask your permission to let me give you my definition. I believe that love has three components and these are:

- Being fully present
- Non-judgement
- Respect

You may have noticed that the first two components (being present and non-judgement) are how I defined happiness. To me, being fully present with someone, without judgement is giving someone your greatest asset—your full attention. You are totally in the other person's world.

Love is a feeling and in essence, it is a feeling of deep connection.

Michael Neill says that you can create a connection with anyone if you spend time with them without your thinking getting in the way. I like to think of this as a bit like 'going on holiday without any luggage'. You are exploring a new place (the other person's world) without your luggage (your beliefs, your past experiences or your worries about the future), so you are exploring the new place with all its beauty, just the way it is.

To me, respect is also a key component of love. I define respect as having due regard for someone's wishes and rights. Everyone has a right to do what they want. Allowing them this freedom seems an important part of expressing love. When your wishes clash with another person's wishes, then you can show love by understanding their wishes and trying to find a middle ground.

KEY INSIGHTS

My definition of love is being fully present, non-judgemental and respectful.

Love is a feeling of deep connection

You can create a connection with anyone when you spend time with them without your thinking getting in the way.

CHAPTER 34

LOVE FOR ALL THINGS LIVING

When it comes to relationships with others, a common theme that causes drama is the idea that 'you' and 'I' are separate. As a result, you can hurt me (and vice versa), when I take your words and your actions personally.

However, if you can see that 'I', 'me' or 'you' only exist in your thinking and that they are not real, then perhaps you can start to see that all living things are connected, they are not separate. Any separation is created by made-up thought. We are all alive, connected and here to experience the present moment, that's it.

What do you mean 'we are all connected'?

Yes, we are all different, but we are not separate. For example, your elbow is different from your wrist, but they are not separate, they are connected (via other body parts). Two people may be different, but they are not separate, except through the made-up thinking of 'me' and 'you'. A human and a tree may be different, but they are not separate, except through made-up labels of 'human' and 'tree'.

All things living are a single energy manifesting in different forms.

I understand that this idea may be difficult to comprehend. Intellectually, you may dismiss it. Remember, your inner judge wants to keep the notion of 'I' alive and it wants to keep it separate, so that there is someone to hurt and someone to take things personally. All I ask is that you sit with this idea, with an open mind, that all things living are connected and see how it makes you feel.

If you can start to see this connection, then you may start to see your experience of life with eyes full of beauty and wonder and gratitude for what we have and respect for everyone and everything.

I am not saying that we all need to become vegans, dressed in organic clothes and sing all day long. I am simply trying to point to the truth that all that exists is the present moment and there is no separation in all things living, except in our thinking.

I have found that walking in nature helps me see this more clearly. When you are immersed in beautiful woodland or taking a walk on a hilltop, it's hard not to be taken aback by the beauty of nature and all things created by Mother Earth and their interconnectedness. In this moment, I find it much easier to be present and grateful for what I have. Hopefully you experience the same.

Something my father taught me was that when you slow down from the business of your daily activities, it becomes easier to see how all things living are connected. He uses the term 'universal consciousness'. Initially, I did not quite understand this, but now I see that he was pointing to the fact that we are all alive and connected. I have found that understanding this makes it easier to love everyone and everything that is alive.

KEY INSIGHTS

All things living are connected, as any separation is created by made-up thoughts.

The concepts of 'I', 'me', or 'you' only exist in thought and are not real.

We are all different, but we are not separate.

All things living are a single energy manifesting in different forms.

Loving everyone becomes easier when you understand that we are all connected.

CHAPTER 35

THE POWER OF FORGIVENESS

Sometimes, people say or do things that appear to be disrespectful. It may be intentional or not, but when we take it personally, we experience feelings such as resentment, anger or upset. Equally, we may act in a disrespectful way to others and this may bring feelings of guilt, or fear of losing this person.

The antidote to eliminating such feelings is forgiveness, of others, or yourself.

Why does it make sense to forgive everyone, including myself?

Forgiveness is not for the other person, forgiveness is for you.

If we do not forgive someone, including ourselves, for a past action or words, then we are the ones that suffer. Without forgiveness, negative feelings can stay with us for days, months, or even years. Holding on to thoughts that create such feelings makes no sense at all.

You may have heard the phrase 'resentment is like taking poison and expecting the other person to die'. Resenting someone is not necessarily going to harm the other person, but it will certainly harm you. If you are giving attention to any resentful thinking, then that is likely to result in negative feelings.

What someone does can seem completely sane to them given what they believe. What they believe might be irrational, but their behaviour seems sane to them. This is another reason why, to me, everything can be forgiven. If we believed what they believed, then our behaviour might be the same.

If you can see that we are all connected, then forgiveness perhaps becomes easier, as forgiving someone else is like forgiving yourself. If you can see that nothing is personal and that nothing is happening 'to you', it is just happening, then you might be able to see that there is nothing or no one to forgive, ever. Whatever justification you use to forgive, it seems that the power of forgiveness is one of the greatest gifts we have to enhance our experience of life.

KEY INSIGHTS

Forgiveness is not for the other person, forgiveness is for you.

Without forgiveness, negative feelings such as resentment, anger and hurt can stay with us.

Resenting someone is not necessarily going to harm the other person, but it will certainly harm you.

When you see that nothing is personal and that nothing is happening 'to you', it is just happening, then it becomes easier to forgive.

FINAL WORDS

As we approach the end of our time together, I would like to reflect on the statements made at the beginning of this book:

- *All (yes, all) the negative emotions in our lives come from made-up thoughts, that do not have to be believed.*

- *Our happiness is built-in and is not linked to what we achieve, do, are or think.*

With an understanding that we are always feeling our thinking, and that thoughts are made-up, I hope that you can see the truth in the first of these statements. Understanding that you do not have to believe your thinking, especially when it is lousy, will disempower your negative thoughts.

And as you start to see and experience the kindness of the design of being human, together with the realisation that our default is happy, you can see the truth in the second statement. Knowing that our happiness is unconditional can set you free to enjoy life fully, with greater peace of mind.

I know that we have covered a lot of material in this book. Some of it may have made sense straight away. You may still be processing other parts. You may even disagree with some of the ideas in the book. All I ask is that you keep an open mind to the possibility that our experience of life, and where our feelings come from, is not as complicated as you think. And once you understand the mechanics - you are feeling your thinking; thoughts are made-up and do not have to be believed; the only truth is whatever is happening right now; and negative feelings come from believing the judge in your head - then you will be able to navigate the rollercoaster of emotions that form our experience of life with a greater sense of ease and enjoyment.

With all my love, Manish

WITH THANKS

The books, authors and people that have influenced me and the content within this book include (but are not limited to):

The Four Agreements by Don Miguel Ruiz. This book described so eloquently four rules which are simple to understand, but perhaps difficult to implement, that can totally transform your life.

The Five Levels of Attachment by Don Miguel Ruiz Jr. This book helped me to understand how having a strong attachment to your beliefs can cause tremendous suffering in our lives.

The Inside Out Revolution by Michael Neill. Introduced me to the understanding that you are 'feeling your thinking at all times' and this forms the backbone to the insights in this book, and the nature of how we experience life.

Loving, What Is by Byron Katie. This book helped me to see more clearly how the only truth is whatever is happening right now.

Life and business strategist Tony Robbins has also been influential in helping me see practical tips for navigating the challenges of day-to-day life.

My father, Anil, for introducing me to various philosophies on life from a young age. He is my guide, my support and one of my best friends.

My mother, Kundan, for showing me, by example, how unconditional love works.

My daughter, Isha, for helping me to stay present, through her innocent joy of life.

My life partner, Dina, for igniting my quest to understand the impact of judgement on our lives and for loving me, no matter what.

Printed in Great Britain
by Amazon

46809485R00119